# THE
# STUDENT
# COOK
# BOOK

First published in Great Britain in 1990
by Collins & Brown Limited
London House
Great Eastern Wharf
Parkgate Road
London SW11 4NQ

A CIP catalogue record for this book
is available from the British Library

9   10   8

ISBN 1 85585 050 8

**Editors**: Felicity Jackson
Sarah Bloxham

**Designer**: Ruth Hope

Typeset by Falcon Graphic Art Ltd,
Wallington, Surrey
Printed and bound in Great Britain
by Cox & Wyman Ltd, Reading

# THE STUDENT COOK BOOK

Eating well without mixer, microwave or money

## Sarah Freeman

COLLINS & BROWN

## ▪ ACKNOWLEDGEMENTS ▪

ABOVE ALL, I want to express my very great thanks to the students who tested these recipes over a long period of time with unflagging energy and enthusiasm. Many more have helped than are named here, but the core of the team was: Polly Freeman, Sydna Younson, Anna Hill, Susila Baybars and Sophie Stewart. In addition, I am deeply grateful to the Ecology Centre, London WC2, Beryl Brownsword, Betty Cadbury-Brown, Marjorie Sheppard, and a number of other people, including those named in the text, for ideas, suggestions and contributions. I also want to thank my husband for his patience on the eating end, and my publishers, notably Gabrielle Townsend, Felicity Jackson, Roger Bristow, Ruth Hope and Sarah Bloxham, not only for patience but encouragement, humour, and generally entering into the spirit of the book.

# ·CONTENTS·

# INTRODUCTION

I know everyone finds introductions boring — but PLEASE READ THIS all the same: it contains essential information. I have made it as short as I can.

The idea of this book originally came from a group of students and has been compiled and researched with their help. They suggested many of the dishes which have been selected and no recipe has been included without being tested by one or more of them and wholeheartedly approved.

Under their guidance, I have made the following assumptions: that readers have little money; little or no previous experience of cooking; only basic cooking equipment; and not necessarily much time. With the odd exception, the only chapter where slightly more elaborate and expensive recipes have been given is in the Parties and Dinner Parties chapter at the back — which is followed by a final chapter on extra cheap dishes for when people are really broke.

## • THE RECIPES •

Up to the chapter on Bread — and several of the kinds of bread almost qualify as meals — all the dishes are intended as main courses, or anyway items which could be eaten as a main course (this applies chiefly to dips and soups). Most are also of the one-dish-per-whole-meal type so that only one needs to be prepared at a time. No one felt that any puddings should be included, since they prefer yoghurt or cheese (although a few suggestions for puddings have been given in the section on Parties and Dinner Parties).

Partly because of prices, which means that even readers who eat meat and fish probably cannot afford it all that often, but also because so many people are now vegetarians, about two-thirds of the dishes (counting bread and cakes) are suitable for the latter: these are marked with a V in the index.

The recipes are accompanied by various comments but I should like to stress that I have desisted from repeating that each one is delicious. If it were not, it would not have been included (apart from my own judgement, the testing team has taken care of that).

In addition, at the risk of being irritating to those who are more experienced, I have explained everything from the beginning. The directions are, therefore, longer than they would otherwise be, but that does not mean that dishes are in any way complicated.

## ▪ HEALTH AND NUTRITION ▪

While good eating has naturally been put first, high priority has also been given to health. Recipes use only as much fat or oil as is necessary for culinary considerations. Butter and cream have been avoided except where really important to taste and consistency (this is for both health and economy) and low- or lower-fat alternatives have been suggested wherever suitable. The same approach has been taken regarding brown rice and flour as opposed to white. All the ingredients specified are fresh with a few virtually inevitable exceptions such as canned tuna fish (but I have not recommended canned tomatoes, although I accept that people will often use them nevertheless).

A few vegetable dishes do not contain much protein: this does not matter provided that the deficiency is recognized and made up for at other times, but vegetarians especially should note that they need an average of 55-85 g of protein a day. Also, because vegetable proteins are less complete than animal proteins, it is a good idea to eat two or more kinds at the same meal (e.g. wheat protein in bread with beans, lentils, and/or nuts). For further details of nutritional needs and a table of food values see page 189.

## ▪ EQUIPMENT ▪

The following have been taken for granted: saucepans, frying pan, grill pan, scales, bowls, a sieve or colander, wire cooling tray and spoons, but nothing else except the means for crushing nuts and herbs. All other items, such as rolling pins, egg whisks, ovenware dishes, and baking trays and tins, have been listed after the ingredients so that they can be begged or borrowed if

necessary. To a large extent, lack of equipment can be overcome: a milk or other bottle will serve as a rolling pin and instead of using scales, one can measure by means of packet sizes or tablespoons:

1 tablespoon sugar or 2 level tablespoons flour = 1 oz/25 g
1 average-sized mug of liquid = ½ pint/300 ml

Elbow-grease and a fork, however, are not sufficient to replace an egg whisk when making meringues; one can put Brazil nuts or walnuts into a (strong) bag and crush them by stamping on them but this will not work for almonds or hazelnuts. It is of course possible to chop nuts with a knife and crush herbs with the back of a spoon, but the one additional piece of· equipment which really is worth having is a pestle and mortar. This unfortunately is expensive but is an investment which will last a life-time (I know this sounds aunt-like, but it is the kind of thing which someone like an aunt might be persuaded to buy as a present).

If you think your oven is inaccurate and the heat is higher than it is supposed to be, allow a few minutes less cooking time or put things near the bottom of the oven and turn them two or three times during cooking.

## · INGREDIENTS ·

Aside from herbs, I have used only items which can be bought in a supermarket or in a few cases a grocer's or health-food shop. Information about ingredients has been given where they occur, but I should like to make two general suggestions. First, dishes will taste infinitely better if sea-salt and black pepper are used, which can either be bought ready-ground or, better still but for which one needs a mill, as coarse crystals or whole corns. Secondly, since fresh herbs are expensive even when obtainable, it is a good idea to grow one's own on the window-sill: the kinds most often needed in this book are parsley, chives, basil, and mint. Starting from seed is cheapest; or one can often buy plants from greengrocers. They will need sun, to be kept moist, and occasional repotting; parsley, chives and mint are hardy but basil needs protection from cold winds and frost and, as an annual, will have to be replaced anyway.

Regarding meat and poultry, I can only say that if one can afford free-range the extra cost is justified not only on humanitarian grounds but also in terms of taste.

## • STORAGE AND HYGIENE •

All animal produce except eggs, i.e. fish, meat, milk and milk products, should be put into the refrigerator as soon as possible (shop on the way home; do not carry them around). Most vegetables should also be stored in the refrigerator: the exceptions are onions, garlic, and potatoes, which simply need to be kept reasonably cool. Potatoes should be kept out of the sun, since bright light sometimes causes them to develop poisonous green patches, which must be peeled off before cooking. If there is a lack of space in the refrigerator, cabbages, carrots, parsnips and turnips will stay fresh in a cool place for several days.

All food stored in the refrigerator should be wrapped or covered with plates and/or food-wrap. Put cooked dishes at the top; uncooked meat at the bottom; vegetables in the salad compartment or near the bottom. Do not place raw and cooked foods (particularly meat) on the same shelf. Most vegetables, cooked meat, stock, and milk can be kept two days; uncooked meat three (but check the sell-by date); cooked vegetable dishes one; commercial yoghurt one or two after the sell-by date;

home-made, four days; fish twelve hours; for cheese, check the best-before date.

Outside the refrigerator, potatoes will keep about 10 days; onions three or four weeks; tomatoes and avocado pears will ripen. Eggs should be eaten within a week of their sell-by date. Dry goods, such as flour, sugar, and pulses will keep for a long time as long as they are kept dry. Flour usually has a best-before date on the packet.

Clean out the refrigerator once a week.

Wash hands after preparing raw meat or vegetables, before starting to cook, and before using them to knead or mix dough or shape biscuits.

## ▪ PREPARATION AND COOKING ▪

Complete directions have been given throughout the book except for a few general points.

To *chop onions* quickly and without their slipping about, cut in half lengthwise to give a flat surface; then place cut-side down, slice, and cross-chop.

To *chop parsley* quickly, gather the leaves into a tight bunch and chop into fine slices across.

To *skin tomatoes*, cover with boiling water and leave for about 30 seconds; unless very underripe, the skin will then peel off easily.

*Vegetables* should be chopped just before you want to use them as they start to lose their vitamins as soon as they are cut. Boil them in only just enough water to cover and then use the cooking water in soups or stocks wherever possible, as more vitamins will have been lost in the cooking water.

To *simmer* means to cook in water which is just on the point of boiling: it moves on the surface or may bubble very slightly, but not vigorously. To achieve this, the heat needs careful adjustment; you also have to remember that if a lid is added, the temperature in the saucepan will rise slightly.

# ·DIPS AND PÂTÉS·

Dips and pâtés can not only be the basis of a meal but are excellent for the odd snack (a bowl of hummus in the refrigerator makes a change from endless bowls of cereal and is a much better idea than chocolate). They are also useful when friends come round and for parties and dinner parties (see page 146).

As well as bread, try serving them with crudités, i.e. raw vegetables such as carrots, courgettes, baby turnips, cauliflower, or celery (which goes particularly with Walnut and Blue Cheese Dip, but not with Tsatziki). Scrub or peel carrots and, unless very new and small, cut in half or thirds across, stand on end, and slit into flat slices or sticks; wash courgettes, removing any damaged or brownish surfaces, and similarly cut into sticks or slices; peel turnips and chop into segments or sticks; cut off a few cauliflower florets, wash and trim off any brown or purple spots (of mould), and chop into bite-sized pieces; trim the root ends and leaves of celery stalks, wash, and chop into convenient lengths.

## · KAITY KARAGEORGIS'S · TSATZIKI

The Karageorgis are Greek friends. Kaity, the mother, is a superb cook whose recipes deserve a book in themselves: I would like to

11

have included more, but many depend on the different state or quality of ingredients in Greece (e.g. fresh olives or sharp-sweet sun-ripened Mediterranean tomatoes).

Be warned: pounded garlic is much more potent than chopped, and although the recipe calls for only one clove, the effect is fairly powerful (as it is meant to be).

In Greece, tsatziki is often served, not with plain bread or toast, but hot slices of bread baked to rusks in a slow oven. *For 4.*

## ▪ INGREDIENTS ▪

| | |
|---|---|
| *3-4 sprigs mint (enough to make 1 tablespoon when chopped)* | *½ pint/300 ml Greek yoghurt* |
| *½ large cucumber* | *1 dessertspoon olive oil* |
| *1 large clove garlic* | *Salt and pepper* |
| *1 teaspoon wine vinegar* | |

## ▪ METHOD ▪

**1** Wash and dry the mint and cucumber (to dry the mint, shake in a colander or drain on kitchen paper).

**2** Peel and roughly chop the clove of garlic, crush to pulp in a pestle and mortar.

**3** Add the vinegar, mix, and stir in the yoghurt and oil.

**4** Pick the mint leaves from the stems and chop finely. Coarsely grate the cucumber into a sieve or colander (to drain off surplus juice). Add to the yoghurt mixture.

**5** Season with salt and pepper, stir, and taste; if desired, add a few drops more vinegar.

# ▪ TABOULEH ▪

Tabouleh is a substantial but refreshing Middle Eastern pâté-type dish based on mint and bulgar wheat (steamed and baked cracked wheat which softens and swells when soaked but needs no further cooking: available from health food shops). Probably as a result of Claudia Roden's classic A *Book of Middle Eastern Food*, it is by now fairly well known in this country. This recipe evolved as a result of a friend's visit to Amman.

The pâté should be left preferably overnight to allow the wheat to swell and the flavours to develop.

If possible, as well as mint, include one or more aromatic herbs such as thyme or marjoram. *For 3-4.*

## • INGREDIENTS •

| | |
|---|---|
| 3-4 sprigs mint (enough for 1 tablespoon when chopped) | 1 large clove garlic |
| | 1 tablespoon olive oil |
| Small bunch mixed herbs, e.g. parsley, chives, thyme, and marjoram (enough for 1 tablespoon when chopped) | 1 tablespoon wine vinegar |
| | 6 oz/190 g bulgar wheat |
| 1 lb/500 g moderately ripe tomatoes | Salt and pepper |

## • METHOD •

**1** Wash and dry the herbs (shake in a colander or drain on kitchen paper). Skin, chop and sieve the tomatoes. (It may seem a waste of time to skin the tomatoes, but they are easily liquified when skinned, leaving only a tablespoon or so of pulp, whereas unskinned ones are extremely difficult to handle.)
**2** Peel, chop, and pound the garlic in a pestle and mortar. Add the oil, vinegar, a little salt, and a generous sprinkling of pepper. Mix with the tomato juice.
**3** Finely chop the herbs and add with the juice to the wheat. Stir, cover, and leave overnight in the refrigerator. Stir again before serving.

# • HUMMUS •

Once the chick peas are cooked, it takes only about 5 minutes to make hummus with a liquidizer; without, at least 20 minutes' energetic sieving or pounding is required (hard work for one person but no great chore if somebody else can take turns).

The proportion of oil used is a matter of preference: the amount can be increased (and that of water decreased) or it can be omitted from the mixture altogether and a film of it poured over the top before serving.

For the best combination of proteins, serve the hummus with bread, pitta bread, or rusks. *For 3-4.*

## • INGREDIENTS •

| | |
|---|---|
| *4 oz/125 g chick peas, soaked overnight* | *1 tablespoon olive oil* |
| *2-3 cloves garlic* | *1 tablespoon tahini* |
| *1 large lemon* | *Salt and black pepper or paprika* |

## • METHOD •

**1** Rinse the soaked peas, pick out any discoloured ones, and put into a saucepan with a little more *un*salted water than is needed to cover them (salt will prevent their softening).

**2** Bring to the boil, skim, and simmer for 1-1½ hours, until they break easily with a fork. Add more water if necessary to keep them covered (keeping up the water level is important not only to ensure that they cook but because some of the liquor is needed for thinning). Drain over a bowl and reserve the liquid.

**3** If *using a liquidizer*: peel and chop the garlic and squeeze the lemon. Add to the peas with the oil, tahini, half a level teaspoon of salt, a sprinkling of the pepper or paprika, and 6 tablespoons of the cooking liquor. Blend until smooth and adjust the seasoning to taste.

**4** If *using a sieve and pestle and mortar*: sieve (or pound) the peas a half or third at a time. Squeeze the lemon. Peel, chop, and crush the garlic in a pestle and mortar and add the peas, lemon juice, tahini, half a level teaspoon of salt, a sprinkling of pepper or paprika, and 4 tablespoons of the cooking liquor (less is needed than when using a liquidizer because the peas are not so finely pulverized and hence less absorbent). Mix, then thin with a little more liquor or oil if required and adjust the seasoning.

**5.** If *using a pestle and mortar alone*: crush the garlic and half the peas at a time, with a little cooking liquor if it makes pounding easier; add lemon juice, tahini, oil, and seasoning as above and enough liquor to give a creamy consistency.

# · WALNUT AND BLUE · CHEESE DIP

Stilton could be used instead of Gorgonzola but I don't recommend it for this recipe as cheaper Stilton sometimes has a soapy taste. *For 4-6*

## · INGREDIENTS ·

| | |
|---|---|
| *4 oz/125 g shelled walnuts or walnut pieces* | *8 oz/250 g ricotta or other soft fresh cheese* |
| *3 oz/90 g Gorgonzola* | *Salt and pepper* |

## · METHOD ·

**1** Roughly crush or finely chop the walnuts (in the absence of a pestle and mortar, put them into a *strong* food bag and crush them with a rolling pin — make sure the edges of the bag are firm and the open end sealed).

**2** Mash the Gorgonzola with a fork.

**3** Season the fresh cheese with a little salt and pepper, add the walnuts and Gorgonzola, and mix thoroughly. If the dip is very stiff, moisten with a little milk or yoghurt. Taste and, if necessary, adjust the seasoning.

# · SMOKED MACKEREL · PÂTÉ

If made with a liquidizer, this comes out a smooth paste; without, it is a moderately rough pâté. Either way (counting washing up the liquidizer), it takes about 7 minutes flat.

Do not be tempted to substitute yoghurt for soured cream: the pâté will not taste the same. *For 4.*

## ▪ INGREDIENTS ▪

| | |
|---|---|
| 12 oz/375 g smoked mackerel fillets | ½ lemon |
| ¼ pint/150 ml soured cream | Pepper |
| 1 medium onion | |

## ▪ METHOD ▪

**1** *If using a liquidizer*: peel and roughly chop the onion. Wipe the mackerel with damp kitchen roll, then skin and break up (the skin pulls off easily); squeeze the lemon. Put into the liquidizer with the cream and a fairly generous seasoning of pepper (no salt) and liquidize until smooth.

**2** *Without a liquidizer*: peel and chop the onion as finely as possible; skin and mash the mackerel with a fork. Mix together, then add the cream, lemon juice, and pepper as above and mash until evenly blended.

# · SOUPS ·

Anyone who doubts whether soup can be sufficiently satisfying to serve as a meal should try Minestrone (see page 26), which is half-way to risotto and will not leave room for anything more than an orange or a few spoonfuls of yoghurt afterwards. Not all the soups in this chapter are quite so filling, but the only ones which might need serious additions to turn them into a meal are Mushroom, and Gazpacho, which is a cold soup intended for consumption in hot weather. Serve them both with crusty bread, though, and you should find them ample.

Most of them are fairly quick to prepare and should not cause you too many headaches as far as method is concerned: Minestrone involves a bit more work but is easy nevertheless and when tested was declared absolutely worth it.

# · Mushroom Soup with · Garlic Croûtons

If large mushrooms are used this soup involves very little preparation (it takes slightly longer if using button mushrooms as they are more fiddly to prepare). A second reason for using large mushrooms is that they tend to have more flavour than smaller ones — buttons often being almost tasteless. (Sometimes, the so-called 'speciality' varieties which are becoming increasingly popular are excellent in terms of flavour — but this is by no means always true and they are often more expensive: in this recipe, if the mushrooms are bland, the garlic will compensate). Use stale bread for the croûtons as it is easier to cut tidily.

As mushrooms do not contain a significant amount of protein, serve with Cheese Bread (page 114) or follow with bread and cheese. *Serves 2-3.*

## ▪ INGREDIENTS ▪

| | |
|---|---|
| *8 oz/250 g mushrooms (large if possible)* | *1 pint/600 ml milk* |
| *2 or 3 cloves garlic* | *½ teaspoon French mustard (e.g. Grey Poupon)* |
| *1 tablespoon olive oil* | *½ teaspoon ground nutmeg* |
| *Salt and pepper* | *2 tablespoons double cream or yoghurt* |
| *1 oz/25 g flour (brown or white; white makes smoother soup but brown is more interesting)* | |

### GARLIC CROÛTONS

| | |
|---|---|
| *1 medium clove garlic* | *1 slice stale bread* |
| *Butter or margarine for spreading* | *Salt and pepper* |

## ▪ METHOD ▪

**1** Chop off the bottoms of the stems, then peel and wipe the mushrooms (or wash button ones, which often cannot be peeled) and dice finely. Peel and finely chop the garlic.

**2** Put into a saucepan with the oil, season with a little salt and rather more pepper, and sweat over a very low flame. At first the mushrooms will soak up all the fat: stir frequently until they exude juice. After 10-15 minutes they will have produced an appreciable quantity and become soft.

**3** Meanwhile, make the croûtons. Peel, chop, and crush the garlic. Mash with the butter or margarine, spread over the bread, then cut into small squares (this means greasy fingers but is easier than the alternative of dotting each square with garlic butter after cutting). Place on a baking sheet and season lightly. Set the oven to 200°C, 400°F, Gas Mark 6.

**4** Add the flour to the mushrooms and stir until incorporated (but do not allow to brown). Gradually pour in the milk, stirring continuously until the soup is smooth. Season lightly again, then simmer very gently, stirring at intervals, for 20 minutes. Ten minutes after adding the milk, put the croûtons into the oven and bake, turning once, for 7-10 minutes until a deep golden.

**5** Just before serving, stir the mustard and nutmeg into the soup, then mix in the cream or yoghurt and taste to see if more seasoning is needed (it is wise to use only a little up to this stage because too much cannot be remedied). Serve the soup with the croûtons handed separately.

# · CELERIAC SOUP ·

This has the consistency of potato soup, but the flavour is much more interesting. Celeriac sometimes turns yellowish when cut; rub your hands with lemon juice if stained.

Use floury potatoes, e.g. King Edward or Cara. *For 4.*

## · INGREDIENTS ·

| | |
|---|---|
| 1 *medium celeriac, weighing* 1¼-1½ *lb/625-750 g* | *Salt and pepper* |
| 1 *lb/500 g potatoes* | ½-¾ *pint/300-450 ml milk* |
| *Small bunch* (½ *oz/15 g or under*) *chives* | 2 *teaspoons French mustard* |
| 1 *pint/600 ml or more water* | 1 *tablespoon double cream* (*optional*) |

## · METHOD ·

**1** Peel and chop the celeriac and potatoes into squares about 1 inch/2.5 cm across. Wash the chives and leave to drain.

**2** Put the celeriac and potatoes into a saucepan with the water (it should just cover them, add a little more if necessary). Season lightly with salt and pepper, bring to the boil and simmer 20 minutes or until tender.

**3** Drain, reserving the water in a bowl, and mash thoroughly with a fork. When the vegetables are smooth and purée-like, stir in the cooking water.

**4** Add ½ pint/300 ml milk, bring to the boil and simmer for 15 minutes more. Remove the milk sediment and stir in the mustard. Chop the chives.

**5** Just before serving, add the cream, if using. Taste and adjust the seasoning, stir again (the solids tend to sink to the bottom), and, if the soup seems too thick, thin with the remaining ¼ pint/150 ml milk. Pour into individual soup plates and sprinkle with chives.

# · LENTIL AND WALNUT SOUP ·

My only reservation about this recipe, which is one of the most interesting for lentils I have tried, is on visual grounds — because it includes soy sauce, the soup turns out, to put it kindly, a not very fortunate brown. I am assured, however, that I am the only person who minds (the addition of yoghurt and more particularly plenty of parsley at the end helps).

The lentils do not need soaking. Serve the soup with crusty brown bread. *For* 3-4.

## · INGREDIENTS ·

| | |
|---|---|
| 2 medium onions | 1¾ pints/1 litre water |
| 2 medium carrots, weighing about 4 oz/125 g | 6 oz/190 g split red lentils |
| Handful of parsley | 6 oz/190 g Greek or Greek-style yoghurt |
| 1 large lemon | Salt and pepper |
| 2 oz/50 g walnuts or walnut pieces | |
| 1 tablespoon each soy sauce and sunflower oil | |

## • METHOD •

**1** Peel and finely chop the onions; scrub or peel and coarsely grate the carrots; wash the parsley and leave to drain. Squeeze the lemon. Roughly crush the walnuts.

**2** Fry the onions gently in the oil for 10 minutes or until soft; add the carrots and fry 5 minutes more, turning constantly. Stir in the walnuts then add the lemon juice, soy sauce, water, and lentils. Bring to the boil and skim. Allow to boil for 10 minutes, turn down the heat, and simmer for 25.

**3** Chop the parsley. If the soup is very thick, add a little more water. Stir in the yoghurt and some of the parsley just before serving. Season to taste with salt and pepper and sprinkle the remaining parsley over the top.

# • FRENCH ONION SOUP •

This is extremely simple — but details make all the difference: the onions need to be fried and the bread and cheese topping baked to just the right degree. *For 4.*

## • INGREDIENTS •

| | |
|---|---|
| 4 large onions, weighing about 1¼-1½ lb/625-750 g | 2 vegetable stock cubes |
| 3 cloves garlic | 2 slices from a large loaf or 4 slices French bread |
| 2 tablespoons oil | 4 oz/125 g Cheddar cheese |
| 1 oz/25 g plain flour | Salt and pepper |
| 3 pints/1¾ litres water | |

## • METHOD •

**1** Peel and finely slice the onions and garlic.

**2** Fry the onions slowly in the oil, turning frequently, for about 15 minutes or until starting to change colour. Add the garlic and fry for 5-8 minutes more or until both are an even light brown — not too light but not dark. Stir in the flour (as this takes up the fat, the result may seem dry). Pour in about ½ pint/300 ml of the water and stir until smooth. Dissolve the stock cubes in 1 pint/ 600 ml boiling water or as directed on the packet. Add with the rest of the water, bring to the boil, and simmer 20-25 minutes.

**3** Set the oven to 200°C, 400°F, Gas Mark 6. Slice the bread fairly thickly and coarsely grate the Cheddar. When the soup has simmered for 10 minutes, put the bread in the oven and bake until golden (7-10 minutes). Sprinkle each slice with some of the cheese and return to the oven for 2-3 minutes or until the cheese has just melted but before it has begun to brown.

**4** Meanwhile, take the soup from the heat and stir in the rest of the cheese. Taste, and season with a little salt and pepper if desired. Pour into serving bowls and add a slice of bread and cheese to each one; submerge briefly before eating.

# · GAZPACHO ·

Like Tabouleh, this is pungent, but refreshing — the more so as it is not a hot soup but served chilled. The best time to make it is August, not only (hopefully) because of the weather, but because it is the cheapest month for cucumbers and tomatoes. *For 3-4*

## · INGREDIENTS ·

| | |
|---|---|
| 2 lb/1 kg medium ripe tomatoes | 3 tablespoons wine vinegar |
| 1 cucumber | 2 tablespoons olive oil |
| 1 large green pepper | ½ teaspoon salt |
| 3-4 cloves garlic | Pepper |
| 2 oz/50 g bread without crust | |

## · METHOD ·

**1** Skin, chop, and sieve the tomatoes into a bowl.

**2** Peel and coarsely grate the cucumber into the tomato juice (because it is tougher than the flesh, the skin tends to resist grating and form ribbons: this applies especially if the cucumber is not very fresh).

**3** Wash and quarter the pepper and remove the core, seeds (which are hot) and white inner flesh. Dice the green flesh into pea-sized squares and add to the tomato and cucumber.

**4** Peel and finely chop the garlic, coarsely grate the bread, then add both to the bowl.

**5** Stir in the vinegar, oil, salt and pepper, then chill for 30 minutes before serving. Taste and add more salt, if necessary.

# · AMERICAN FISH · CHOWDER

This chowder is a real meal in itself — it doesn't even need crusty bread. It is an American classic based on a recipe originally published in *The Boston Cooking-School Cook Book* by Fannie Farmer, the American equivalent to Mrs Beeton.

If possible, choose floury potatoes (King Edward, Cara, Pentland Squire or Romano). *For 3-4.*

## · INGREDIENTS ·

| | |
|---|---|
| 12 oz/375 g fresh or frozen cod or haddock fillets | 4 oz/125 g streaky bacon |
| 1-1¼ lb/500-625 g potatoes | ½ oz/15 g butter, plus oil |
| Salt and pepper | 1 teaspoon plain flour |
| 3 cloves garlic | 1-1½ pints/600-900 ml milk |
| 1 large or 2 small onions | **Large and medium saucepans** |

## · METHOD ·

**1** Skin the fish if necessary. Pull the skin sharply from one corner; if it sticks, ease it off with a knife. Scrub or peel and slice the potatoes (scrubbing or peeling is a matter of choice; unpeeled potatoes provide more fibre and vitamin C, but if they disintegrate, the soup will contain strips of unattached peel. In either case, peel off any very green patches).

**2** Cut fresh fish into chunks and check for bones. Cover with water in the smaller saucepan, season lightly with salt, bring to the boil, skim, and simmer until it flakes when prodded with a fork (7-12 minutes according to thickness). Poach frozen fish for as long as it says on the packet. Drain in a sieve or colander over the larger saucepan.

**3** Boil the potato slices in the saucepan of fish liquid, adding water to cover, for 10-15 minutes or until just soft.

**4** Peel and chop the garlic and onion; remove rind from the bacon and dice (use scissors). Fry the onion and bacon slowly in the butter and oil for 10 minutes or until soft; add the garlic and fry for 5 minutes or until the onion begins to change colour. Stir in the flour, add half the milk, and simmer for 2-3 minutes. When thickened, add to the potato with the remaining milk.

**5** Simmer the milk and potato mixture just long enough for the potatoes to start to crumble (5-10 minutes), then add the fish. Season moderately with salt and fairly generously with pepper, and continue simmering for a further 2 or 3 minutes. Taste and adjust the seasoning (both more salt and pepper may be needed) and serve.

# · SCOTTISH MUTTON AND · BARLEY SOUP

This is based on stock made with the bone left over from Lamb Kebabs with Fennel and Lamb with Aubergine (see pages 75 and 77) and in its own way is quite as good as either and almost as filling.

The stock, which needs to be made in advance, should be boiled as soon as the lamb has been boned (let it simmer while the main dish is cooking) and can be kept for 2 days in the refrigerator. In fact, if reboiled it could be kept for another 2 but the meat which goes with it should be used as soon as possible while it is still succulent and tender.

The basic recipe is a British classic: the version I have chosen to include here is a loose adaptation from the *Constance Spry Cookery Book*. For 4.

## • INGREDIENTS •
### STOCK

| | |
|---|---|
| 1 carrot | 1 lamb bone |
| 1 onion | 3 pints/1¾ litres water |
| 1 bayleaf | Salt and pepper |
| Sprig of fresh parsley and thyme or a pinch of dried thyme or mixed herbs | **Large saucepan, preferably with a lid** |

### SOUP

| | |
|---|---|
| Stock | 2 sticks celery |
| 2oz/50g pearl barley | 2 leeks |
| ½ pint/300 ml water | Meat from the lamb bone |
| 2 large carrots | Salt and pepper |

## • METHOD •

**1** First make the stock. Peel and roughly slice the carrot and onion and put into the saucepan with the other ingredients, seasoning lightly with salt and pepper. Bring to the boil, then lower the heat to simmering point (i.e. just under boiling, when the water barely bubbles), cover, and cook for 1½ hours.

**2** Pour through a sieve into a bowl and leave until cool enough to handle. Throw away the vegetables but keep any detached pieces of meat. Pick or cut the meat from the bone, discarding fat and gristle; do not return to the stock, but place in a separate bowl. Cover both meat and stock with plates, leave to cool, then put into the refrigerator.

**3** Remove the solidified fat from the top of the stock. Pour the liquid into a saucepan and add the barley. Bring to the boil and simmer for just over an hour (about 70 minutes). As by then the level of liquid will have been reduced by evaporation and the absorbency of the barley, add up to ½ pint of water.

**4** Meanwhile, peel and slice the carrots. Cut the leaves and any brown patches from the celery, then wash, and slice finely. Trim the roots and leaves from the leeks, peel off the outer layer, slice very finely and rinse in a colander under the tap (this ensures that mud between the layers is removed). Chop the meat into small cubes or squares.

**5** Add the prepared meat and vegetables plus a pinch of salt and pepper and ½ pint/300 ml water to the contents of the saucepan and continue simmering for 20 minutes more. Taste before serving and if necessary add more seasoning.

# · MINESTRONE ·

There are many variations of minestrone, some made with meat and some with vegetables only — the former being incomparably more interesting. The essential element, which lifts it from undistinguished vegetable soup, is bacon — just a very little being all that is needed. Another ingredient which enriches it enormously is Chicken Stock (see page 28). The accompanying chicken meat can either be added or, if there is enough, used for Chicken in Béchamel (see page 86).

Even more than American Fish Chowder, this is a meal in itself. Crusty bread goes with it particularly well but it would be a pity to eat too much of it at the expense of the soup, which contains rice and is better not kept because the grains absorb so much liquid that what started as minestrone ends up more like risotto.

The stock should be made when the chicken is cut up (or, if it has been roasted, within 24 hours) but can be kept for 2 days in the refrigerator. The soup requires 2½ hours cooking before the rice is added, and can be prepared in advance up to this point.

Use a floury potato, e.g. King Edward, Pentland Squire or Cara. *For* 4-6.

## ▪ INGREDIENTS ▪

| | |
|---|---|
| 2 oz/50 g streaky bacon | 1 medium potato weighing about 8 oz/250 g |
| 1 medium onion | |
| 2-3 cloves garlic | 2 large or 3 medium carrots, weighing about 8 oz/250 g |
| 1 lb/500 g ripe tomatoes | |

| | |
|---|---|
| 2 or 3 sticks celery | Chicken meat from the carcass (optional) |
| 4 oz/125 g white kidney beans | |
| 3½ pints/just over 2 litres Chicken Stock (see page 28) and/or water | 2-3 oz/50-90 g grated Parmesan cheese |
| 3 largish cabbage leaves | Crusty bread, for serving |
| 2 tablespoons oil, if necessary | **Large saucepan** |
| Salt and pepper | |
| 3 oz/90 g brown Italian or long-grain rice | |

## ▪ METHOD ▪

**1** Cut rind from the bacon and dice (use scissors); peel and finely chop the onion, garlic, potato, and carrots. Peel and chop the tomatoes; trim the root and leaf ends of the celery, wash, and finely chop; rinse the beans.

**2** Skim the fat, which will have solidified, from the top of the stock and put about 1 oz/25 g into the saucepan; if there is insufficient or stock is not being used, replace it with up to 2 tablespoons of oil. Fry the bacon and onion over very low heat, turning often, for 10-15 minutes or until the onion is just beginning to change colour. Add the garlic and continue frying for 5 more minutes.

**3** Add the tomato and continue frying, pressing the flesh against the sides of the pan, for a further 15 minutes or until a smooth sauce is formed. Put in the stock or water, beans, and the rest of the prepared vegetables, season with a little pepper but not salt, and boil briskly for 10 minutes. Lower the heat and simmer for 1¾ hours. (At this point the soup may be left for serving later.)

**4** Bring to simmering point, if necessary, add the rice and a little salt, and simmer for 20 minutes. Wash, shred, and add the cabbage. If chicken meat is to be included, remove any skin and fat, dice the meat, including the liver, and stir in. Simmer for 10 minutes more or until the rice is tender. Taste and adjust the seasoning, but remember that the soup will be accompanied by Parmesan cheese, which is salty. Serve with the grated Parmesan and crusty bread.

# · CHICKEN STOCK ·

This is a great improvement ingredient in soups such as Minestrone (see page 26) and also many other dishes, particularly rice dishes like Chicken Risotto and Chicken Pilaff (see pages 47 and 49) and those where rice is an accompaniment.

## · INGREDIENTS ·

| | |
|---|---|
| 1 chicken carcass plus, if the chicken is uncooked, the liver | 2½-3 pints/1½-1¾ litres water |
| | Salt and pepper |
| 1 carrot | **Large saucepan, if possible with a lid** |
| 1 onion | |
| 1 bay leaf | |
| Sprig parsley and thyme or a pinch of dried thyme or mixed herbs | |

## · METHOD ·

**1** An uncooked carcass is preferable but the remains of a roast chicken can also be used, in which case cut off all the meat before starting.

**2** Scrub or peel the carrot and slice coarsely; peel and roughly slice or quarter the onion; wash fresh herbs. Remove fat from the chicken liver and rinse in cold water. Put all the ingredients into the saucepan, seasoning sparingly with salt and pepper; if the water covers less than about three-quarters of the carcass, add a little more. Bring to the boil, lower the heat, put on the lid, and simmer a raw carcass for 1 hour (a cooked one will need simmering for 4-5 hours).

**3** Strain the stock into a bowl. With a pre-roasted carcass, throw away both bones and vegetables. With a fresh one, leave until it is cool enough to handle and strip; the meat will be perfectly cooked and much more tender than if roasted. When the stock is cold, cover and refrigerate; the meat and liver should be put on a plate and similarly covered and refrigerated when cold.

# · PASTA ·

FRESH PASTA is becoming increasingly easy to buy — but unfortunately is about three times as expensive as the dried (packet) version. In my view, this about represents its gastronomic superiority: also, fresh pasta has the advantage of saving time, since it takes only 3-5 rather than 20 minutes to boil or, in the case of lasagne, does not need boiling at all. Some forms of dried lasagne also do not need boiling, but you must remember to add more liquid to the sauce or the finished dish will be dry.

Probably nobody needs to be warned about the meanness of serving quantities on packet labels; pasta shops, on the other hand, sometimes err in the other direction and recommend unrealistically large amounts. Allow 4-5 oz/125-160 g of dried or 5-6 oz/160-190 g of fresh per head.

Fresh pasta will stay moist for up to 24 hours in the refrigerator but thereafter will start to dry out.

Use plenty of water to cook pasta. Put the pasta into boiling salted water, feeding in dried spaghetti gradually so that it curls round the saucepan. Turn the heat up full until the water is brought back to the boil, and then simmer for as long as directed on labels or by the shop (fresh tagliatelli takes 3 minutes, fresh shells 5). The pasta is ready as soon as it can be cut with a blunt knife. Drain immediately, shake, not only to remove surplus water but also to prevent sticking, add a knob of butter or a little oil (again, this will help to prevent sticking) and serve as quickly as possible.

# · TOMATO SAUCE ·

Few things are more delicious than sauce made with sweet, tangy, sun-ripened tomatoes, the freshness of which would be spoilt by the addition of paste. However, as most tomatoes now available taste of very little, paste is recommended to strengthen their flavour. Nor are canned ones a satisfactory answer: resort to them if you must for composite dishes but do not use them in sauce which is to be served *per se*.

Just as firm, sharper tomatoes are preferable for salads, so ripe, softer ones are more suitable for sauce, not only in terms of texture and acidity but because they are easier to skin. *For 3-4.*

## ▪ INGREDIENTS ▪

| | |
|---|---|
| *1 ½ lb/75 g ripe tomatoes* | *1 tablespoon oil* |
| *1 medium onion* | *Salt and pepper* |
| *2-3 cloves garlic* | *1 tablespoon tomato paste* |
| *A few sprigs parsley* | *⅛ pint/80 ml water* |

## ▪ METHOD ▪

**1** Peel and chop the tomatoes, removing the core. Peel and finely chop the onion and garlic. Wash the parsley and leave to drain on kitchen paper.
**2** Fry the onion in the oil over gentle heat for 7-10 minutes until soft. Add the garlic and continue frying for 5 more minutes or until the onion is just beginning to change colour.
**3** Add the tomatoes, season with salt and pepper, and simmer for 10 minutes, pressing out larger lumps of tomato flesh against the sides of the pan. Dissolve the paste in the water and stir in. Continue cooking for 5 more minutes or until the sauce is smooth and thick. Finely chop and add the parsley.

# · QUICK CHIVE SAUCE ·

As this sauce is fairly pungent, a tablespoon per serving is as much as is needed. It can be made in about 5 minutes — less time than it takes to bring the water to the boil and cook fresh pasta. *For 4.*

## · INGREDIENTS ·

| | |
|---|---|
| About ½ oz/15 g (small handful) chives | ¼ pint/150 ml double cream |
| 1 clove garlic | 2 teaspoons French mustard |
| 4 oz/125 g ricotta, curd, or other soft cheese | Salt and pepper |
| | Grated parmesan cheese, to serve |

## · METHOD ·

**1** Wash, shake dry, and finely chop the chives.
**2** Peel the clove of garlic and crush to a purée in a pestle and mortar.
**3** Beat the soft cheese into the garlic; then add all the other ingredients, except the Parmesan cheese, and season the mixture with salt and pepper to taste. Do not heat, but simply place a dollop on top of each plate of hot pasta. Serve the Parmesan cheese separately.

# · PESTO ·

Just as Roquefort has been said to be the king of cheeses, so pesto can be called the queen of sauces. It is absurdly expensive to buy but with home-grown basil fairly cheap to make — and very easy. The snag is that because a lot of basil is needed, it cannot be made very often or for many people from one small plant. For this reason, the quantities given are for only 2. To help the plant to recover, pick the underneath rather than the new top leaves. *For 2.*

## • INGREDIENTS •

| | |
|---|---|
| About 16 basil leaves | 2 small or 1 large clove garlic |
| 2 or 3 fat sprigs parsley (these are not necessary for flavour but help to stretch the basil) | 1 oz/25 g pine nuts |
| | 2 tablespoons olive oil |
| 1 oz/25 g Parmesan cheese | Salt and pepper |

## • METHOD •

**1** Wash, shake dry, and roughly chop the basil and parsley. Finely grate the Parmesan, if necessary.

**2** Crush the garlic in a pestle and mortar.

**3** Add all the other ingredients to the mortar except salt and pepper and 1 tablespoonful of the oil (if the full quantity of oil is put in at this stage, pounding is more difficult because it tends to splatter). Pound to a thick paste.

**4** Season with a little salt and slightly more pepper. Stir in the rest of the oil. The sauce is now ready — it does not require cooking or heating. It settles if left to stand, so mix before serving.

# • MEAT SAUCE •

In addition to being served as a sauce in its own right, this is the conventional filling for lasagne. As with minestrone, one essential element to its success is bacon; another is long, slow simmering. This may seem a bore, but it transforms mere mince into a rich-tasting ragù (to use the Italian term). It is convenient, however, in that it can be made the previous day and once all the ingredients are added (except yoghurt, which is stirred in at the end) needs no attention whatsoever.

Wine adds to the flavour but is not essential. *For 4-6.*

## • INGREDIENTS •

| | |
|---|---|
| 4 oz/125 g (4 long rashers) streaky bacon | 1 medium onion |

| | |
|---|---|
| 3 cloves garlic | ½ teaspoon dried mixed herbs |
| 8oz/250 g (3-4) ripe tomatoes | 2 tablespoons tomato paste |
| 1 small carrot | Small glass red wine (optional) plus ½ pint/300 ml water or ¾ pint/ 450 ml water |
| 1 large stick celery | |
| 1 tablespoon oil, preferably olive | 1 tablespoon Greek or Greek-style yoghurt |
| 1 lb/500 g finely minced lean beef | |
| Salt and pepper | **Largish saucepan with a lid** |

### • METHOD •

**1** Trim the rind from the bacon and dice finely (use scissors). Peel and finely chop the onion and garlic; skin and chop the tomatoes, discarding the cores; peel and dice the carrot; wash and dice the celery, scraping off any brownish patches.

**2** Fry the onion and bacon in the oil over low heat, turning frequently, for 10 minutes or until soft. Stir in the carrot, celery, and garlic and fry for another 5 minutes. Add the meat, season lightly with salt and moderately with pepper, and continue frying, turning continuously, until it is brown all through, with no raw pockets where it has stuck into lumps.

**3** Sprinkle with the dried herbs and stir in the tomatoes, pressing the flesh smooth against the sides and bottom of the pan (make a hole in the meat if necessary). Mix the tomato paste with the water and pour in, then add the wine if using. Put the lid on the saucepan and leave to simmer for 2 hours.

**4** If being made in advance, turn into a bowl, cover, leave to cool, then put into the refrigerator. To serve, bring to the boil and simmer for a further 10 minutes. Remove the sauce from the heat before stirring in the yoghurt. Serve at once.

# • LASAGNE •

Although lasagne is traditionally made with meat sauce, any number of vegetable and other fillings are possible (for Aubergine Lasagne, see page 36).

The amount of pasta needed will depend on the width of the dish: 10 oz/310 g is plenty for the size specified (in fact, with no overlapping, one could just manage with 8 oz/250 g) but it may take 12 oz/375 g to fill a larger one.

Most dried lasagne needs boiling before using in this dish but lasagne that needs no pre-cooking is now readily available; if you use this you may need to add an extra ¼ pint/150 ml of liquid to the sauce. Fresh lasagne can be used directly. Any sort, i.e. white, brown, or flavoured (tomato or spinach) is suitable.

Either the main part of the filling or the complete dish can be prepared the previous day. *For 5-6.*

## ▪ INGREDIENTS ▪

| | |
|---|---|
| 6 oz/190 g (6 long rashers) streaky bacon | Salt and pepper |
| 1 large or 2 small onions | Level teaspoon dried mixed herbs |
| 4 cloves garlic | 3 tablespoons tomato paste |
| 12 oz/375 g (5-6) ripe tomatoes | ½ glass red wine (optional) plus ¼ pint/150 ml water or ½ pint/ 300 ml water |
| 1 large carrot | |
| 1 large or 2 smaller sticks celery | 10 oz/310 g lasagne |
| 1½ tablespoons oil, preferably olive | A little grated Parmesan cheese for sprinkling |
| 1½ lb/750 g finely minced, lean beef | |

### BÉCHAMEL SAUCE

| | |
|---|---|
| 1½ pints/900 ml milk | 2 oz/50 g brown or white flour (white gives a smoother sauce; brown goes better with brown lasagne but slightly masks the cheese) |
| Bay leaf (optional) | |
| 2 oz/50 g Parmesan cheese | |
| 1 oz butter plus 2 tablespoonfuls oil or 4 tablespoonsful oil | **Large saucepan with a lid** |
| ½ teaspoonful nutmeg | **Ovenware dish 10 inches/ 25 cm across and 3-4 inches/ 8-10 cm deep** |
| Salt and pepper | |

## • METHOD •

**1** Snip the rind from the bacon and dice finely (use scissors). Peel and chop the onion(s) and garlic; skin and chop the tomatoes, cutting out the cores. Peel and dice the carrot; wash and dice the celery, removing any brownish surfaces.

**2** Fry the onion and bacon slowly in 1½ tablespoons oil, turning frequently, for 10 minutes or until soft. Stir in the garlic, celery, and carrot, and fry for 5 minutes more. Add the meat, season with a little salt and a moderate amount of pepper, and continue frying, turning continuously, until all parts of the meat are browned. Sprinkle with the herbs and stir in the tomatoes, pressing out lumps of flesh against the bottom of the pan (make a hole in the meat). Mix the tomato paste with the water and pour in, then add the wine. Put the lid on the pan and leave to simmer for 2 hours.

**3** About 20 minutes before the end of the cooking time, cook the pasta, if necessary, and make the béchamel sauce. (The béchamel takes about 15 minutes. Time it so that the sauce is ready before the pasta — it is important to assemble the lasagne as soon as the pasta is cooked because the sheets will stick together if allowed to cool.)

**4** To make the béchamel sauce, heat, but do not boil, the milk with the bay leaf, if using (heating extracts the flavour of the leaf but is helpful even without one because the sauce thickens more quickly if the milk is hot). Grate the cheese if necessary. Melt the butter over gentle heat in 2 tablespoons oil, or warm 4 tablespoons oil in a saucepan or large frying pan. Add the flour and mix until smooth (it is important not to allow it to brown). Remove the bay leaf and pour in the milk, stirring continuously, then continue to stir until the sauce is thick. Add the nutmeg, season moderately with salt and pepper, and simmer for about 3 minutes. Stir in the Parmesan cheese. Set the oven to 200°C, 400°F, Gas Mark 6.

**5** Spread one-third of the meat over the bottom of the ovenware dish. Pour over slightly less than one-quarter of the béchamel sauce, sprinkle with a little extra grated Parmesan cheese and cover with a layer of pasta. Repeat twice and finish with a thickish layer of sauce. (If made in advance, allow to cool, cover, and put into the refrigerator.) Bake for 25-30 minutes or until the top is beginning to brown.

# · AUBERGINE LASAGNE ·

Choose aubergines that are hard and shiny; flabbiness or wrinkling means that they are stale (slight brown markings on the inside around the seeds, however, are not streaks of mould). Courgettes should similarly be glossy and hard, without shrivelling at the end; the smaller they are, the better their flavour will be so opt for these if given the choice.

If possible, leave both to sweat for an hour after slicing; this is not absolutely necessary but draws out some of their moisture, which in the case of aubergines is sometimes slightly bitter, and reduces their absorbency so that less oil is needed for grilling or frying (fried aubergines demand so much oil, and preferably olive rather than cheaper oil, that grilling is recommended wherever possible). Again, add extra water if you are using no-cook lasagne. *For 5-6.*

## · INGREDIENTS ·

| | |
|---|---|
| 1¼ lb/625 g aubergines (2 smallish or 1 large) | About 3 tablespoons oil |
| Salt, some of which should be finely ground | Pepper |
| | 1½ tablespoons tomato paste |
| 1 medium onion | Béchamel sauce (see Lasagne) |
| 3 cloves garlic | ⅛ pint/80 ml water |
| 1½ lb/750 g ripe tomatoes | 10 oz/310 g lasagne |
| A few sprigs fresh or 1 teaspoon dried rosemary | A little extra Parmesan cheese |
| 1 red pepper | **Frying pan or large saucepan with a lid** |
| 1¼ lb/625 g courgettes | **10 inch/25 cm ovenware dish** |

## · METHOD ·

**1** Wash the aubergine(s) and chop into ¼ inch/0.5 cm slices. Sprinkle each slice with a little fine salt and leave to sweat in a colander for an hour. Rinse under the tap, shake off surplus water, and allow to drain.

**2** Peel and chop the onion, garlic, and tomatoes, discarding the hard tomato cores. Wash fresh rosemary; strip the leaves from the stems, reject any blackened ones, and chop into short lengths. Wash, quarter, and dice the pepper, throwing away the core; cut out the white inner flesh and any discoloured spots; pick off all seeds (which are hot). Wash the courgettes, pare off any damaged or discoloured surfaces, then cut into ⅓ inch/1 cm slices. Sprinkle with salt and leave to sweat in a sieve, or simply spread out on a plate. (If making the aubergine sauce in advance, prepare the courgettes an hour before continuing with the rest of the recipe.)

**3** Cover the bottom of the frying pan or saucepan with 1 tablespoon of the oil and fry the onion over gentle heat for 10 minutes or until soft. Add the garlic and pepper and fry for 5 minutes more. Add the aubergine and tomatoes, seasoning slightly with salt and moderately with pepper. Cover and simmer for 15 minutes. Mix the tomato paste with the water and add; very gently turn the vegetables, making sure that the aubergine is submerged in liquid. Continue simmering for another 15 minutes or until the aubergine is soft. (If the sauce is being made in advance, transfer to a bowl, leave to cool, cover, and put into the refrigerator.)

**4** Rinse the courgette slices and dry with kitchen roll. Fry fairly briskly in about 2 tablespoons of oil until pale gold on both sides. Put on a plate lined with kitchen paper to absorb surplus fat. Set the oven to 200°C, 400°F, Gas Mark 6.

**5** Cook the pasta, if necessary; make the béchamel sauce, timing the sauce to be ready before the pasta (see Lasagne: page 33).

**6** Arrange the aubergine sauce, courgettes, béchamel, extra cheese, and pasta in three layers, leaving a thick fourth layer of béchamel for the top. (If making in advance, leave to cool, cover and refrigerate.) Bake for 25-30 minutes or until the top begins to turn brown. Follow packet instructions if using no-boil dried lasagne.

# · PASTRY ·

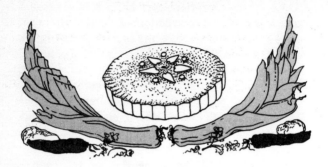

GOOD PASTRY has to contain a high proportion of fat: the best way to compensate for this is to roll it thinly.

Any kind of fat or oil can be used, but a mixture of butter and lard, or pastry made with cream according to the recipe below are the easiest to handle. It is a good idea to put all pastry dough (except that made with oil, which, since the latter will not solidify, does not respond in the same way) into the refrigerator to cool before rolling it out. This applies particularly if margarine, which reacts relatively quickly to warmth, is used. The dough can be made the previous day and left in the fridge overnight, but in that case will need a few minutes to soften.

Generally speaking, plain flour gives a crisper result than self-raising; although wholemeal alone makes excellent pastry, it is easier to handle when used in combination with white.

There are several types of pastry and many variations within them: directions for *choux* pastry, which contains eggs and does not involve rolling, are included in recipes where it is needed, but otherwise the following are sufficient for most purposes.

Three maxims: keep dough cool; add liquid sparingly, since if it is too wet the pastry will be tough; and (the opposite to bread dough) work it as little as possible — in other words, be lazy.

As well as the recipes here, one sweet tart is given in Cakes and Tarts (Brown Bread Treacle Tart with Lemon: see page 141), and Lamb, Kidney and Mushroom Pie and Spinach and Pine Nut Tart in Parties and Dinner Parties (see pages 148 and 158).

# · SHORTCRUST PASTRY ·

## · INGREDIENTS ·

| | |
|---|---|
| 6 oz/190 g flour, either white or 3 oz/90 g white and 3 oz/90 g wholemeal | White flour for dusting |
| | Salt |
| 2 oz/50 g butter plus 1 oz/25 g lard or 3 oz/90 g margarine, chilled | Rolling pin (or a clean milk or beer bottle) |
| 2 tablespoons cold water | Board/surface for rolling out |

## · METHOD ·

**1** Chop the fat into pieces about ⅓ inch/1 cm square. Mix the flours and salt.

**2** Add the flour to the fat and rub in the fat with your fingertips until the mixture is like breadcrumbs. Measure in 1½ tablespoons of the water and form the mixture into a ball, gradually adding the rest of the water, if needed. Press it gently into a firm but cohesive lump: if it seems at all sticky, shake a little extra white flour over it. Cool if possible.

**3** Generously dust the rolling pin and board or surface with white flour and set ready the tart, pie, or baking dish. Roll firmly but quickly into a sheet about ¼ inch/0.5 cm thick; if it crumbles or breaks, gather it up, scatter more flour over the rolling pin and surface, and re-roll. Small cracks or breaks which appear after the dish is covered can be patched with trimmings, which should be dampened on the underside to ensure that they stick.

# · DOUGH MADE WITH CREAM ·

Although this tends to be tough when used *per se* and is more expensive than conventional short pastry, it is quicker to make, much easier to roll out, and yields exceptionally crisp brown-flour flaky pastry.

As precise proportions matter, relatively accurate metric equivalents rather than convenient approximations are given.

## • INGREDIENTS •

| | |
|---|---|
| 2 oz/60 g white flour | ¼ pint/140 ml double cream |
| 2 oz/60 g granary or wholemeal flour | Salt |

## • METHOD •

**1** Mix together the flours and salt.

**2** Make a well in the centre and pour in the cream. Work into dough, first with a spoon, then with the hands. The thickness of cream varies: very thick cream will need more working than thinner. Press into a ball and cool if possible before rolling out.

# • FLAKY PASTRY •

## • INGREDIENTS •

| | |
|---|---|
| 1 quantity of Shortcrust Pastry or Dough Made with Cream | White flour for sprinkling and dusting |
| 2 oz/50 g butter or margarine, straight from the fridge | |

## • METHOD •

**1** Cut the butter into 8 thin slices.

**2** Dust the rolling pin and board with flour and roll the dough into a thick oblong. Sprinkle generously with flour, place 2 slices of butter on one half of it, and fold into a square. Roll into another oblong and repeat 3 more times.

**3** Set the pie or tart dish ready, flour the pin and board, and roll out as for shortcrust pastry.

# Cheese and
# · Vegetable Tart ·

This is not quite like a quiche because it contains more vegetables and the cheese tends to form a sauce instead of setting.

The sauce can be made with curd or other medium-fat soft cheese, cream, or a mixture (cheese is healthier; cream improves the texture). Choose a cauliflower which is white and creamy all over with no patches of brown or purple mould. *For 4.*

## · INGREDIENTS ·

| | |
|---|---|
| 2 large carrots, weighing about 8 oz/250 g | 2 eggs, size 2 or 3 |
| 2 medium leeks | Pepper |
| Salt | 4 oz/125 g strong (Farmhouse) Cheddar cheese |
| ½ medium cauliflower | 1 quantity Shortcrust Pastry with half wholemeal flour or Flaky Pastry using Dough Made with Cream |
| 2 large or 3 medium heads broccoli, weighing about 8 oz/250 g | |
| 4 oz/125 g curd cheese plus 2 tablespoons milk or ¼ pint/ 150 ml double cream | 8½ inch/22 cm tart dish |
| | Saucepan with a lid |

## · METHOD ·

1 Scrub or peel and slice the carrots fairly thinly. Chop the leaves and roots from the leeks and cut into thicker (about ⅓ inch/1 cm) slices; wash and rinse in a colander under the cold tap. Put both into the saucepan, just cover with water, add a little salt, and bring to the boil. Cook, uncovered, over gentle heat for 10 minutes.

2 Meanwhile, divide the cauliflower lengthwise and store the part not needed in a food bag in the refrigerator. Wash and cut into florets about ½ inch/1.5 cm across. Wash and cut broccoli into florets the same size. Lay them over the leeks and carrots,

sprinkle with a very little more salt, put on the saucepan lid, and boil briskly for 5 minutes. They will not be covered with water but will cook in the steam (which is often a much better way of cooking vegetables than boiling as it does not leach them of their nutrients). After 5 minutes, all the items in the saucepan should be just tender but still crisp. Drain thoroughly.

**3** Set the oven to 200°C, 400°F, Gas Mark 6. If curd cheese is being used, beat the eggs into the cheese one at a time; thin with the milk when smooth. With cream, beat the eggs together before adding the cream. Season lightly with salt and more generously with pepper; grate and stir in the Cheddar.

**4** Line the tart dish with the pastry. Arrange the vegetables evenly in the bottom, pour over the cheese mixture, making sure that it coats them all, and bake for 25 minutes or until the top is golden. Serve immediately.

# · CARROT AND WALNUT · TART

Although the tart is not sweet, the taste of the carrots is accentuated by nutmeg, cinnamon, and raisins. To allow the flavours to develop, eat cold (as it has a firm texture, it is particularly suitable for picnics and packed meals). *For 6.*

## · INGREDIENTS ·

| | |
|---|---|
| 1¼ lb/625 g carrots | 2 eggs, size 2 |
| Salt and pepper | 8 oz/250 g medium fat soft cheese |
| Small handful parsley (enough for 1 tablespoon when chopped) | ¼ teaspoon ground nutmeg |
| | ¼ teaspoon ground cinnamon |
| 1 medium onion | 1 quantity Flaky Pastry made with cream |
| 2-3 cloves garlic | |
| 5 oz/160 g walnuts or walnut pieces | 8½ inch/22 cm tart dish |
| 1 oz/25 g raisins | |

## • METHOD •

**1** Peel the carrots, cover with slightly salted water, and boil 25 minutes or until tender. Drain and mash. Meanwhile, wash the parsley and leave to drain.

**2** Peel and finely chop the onion and garlic; coarsely crush the nuts (a few largish pieces add interest to the texture); finely chop the parsley. Add with the raisins to the cooked carrots. Set the oven to 180°C, 350°F, Gas Mark 4.

**3** Beat the eggs into the cheese (rather than the other way round) and add the nutmeg and cinnamon, a little salt, and a fairly generous amount of pepper.

**4** Line the tart dish with the pastry.

**5** Stir the carrot mixture into the cheese and egg, turn into the pastry case, and bake for 30-35 minutes until the top is just beginning to change colour. Leave to cool before serving.

# • LEEK AND SMOKED • HADDOCK QUICHE

An almost infinite variety fo fillings can be used for quiches: this one is a particularly good combination of flavours.

The haddock is baked rather than boiled for maximum flavour. Cream improves the texture of the filling but is not necessary; if it is used, a little extra Parmesan cheese is recommended to maintain flavour. The pastry, leeks, and fish can be prepared in advance. For 4-6.

## • INGREDIENTS •

| | |
|---|---|
| 1 lb/500 g leeks | 8 oz/250 g medium-fat curd cheese |
| Salt and pepper | |
| 8-10 oz/250-310 g filleted smoked haddock | 1 oz/25 g Parmesan cheese or if using cream 1½ oz/40 g |
| 4 tablespoons milk | ⅛ pint/80 ml double cream (optional) |
| 4 eggs, size 2 or 3 | |

| | |
|---|---|
| 1 *quantity Shortcrust Pastry or Flaky Pastry using Dough Made with Cream* (*see page* 39) | **8½ inch/22 cm tart dish** |

## ▪ METHOD ▪

**1** Set the oven to 180°C, 350°F, Gas Mark 4. Chop the leaves and roots from the leeks and cut into moderately thick (about ⅓ inch/1 cm) slices. Wash, separating the layers if mud is caught between them, and rinse under the tap in a colander. Bring to the boil with a pinch of salt and cook over medium heat for 15 minutes or until just soft. Leave to cool.

**2** Meanwhile, rinse the haddock in cold water and skin if necessary. Raise the skin at one edge and pull sharply: scrape off any flesh which clings to it with a knife. Place in a small ovenware dish with the milk, cover (not only to prevent drying but the smell from escaping into the oven) and bake for 15-20 minutes or until it can be separated with a fork. Drain but keep the cooking liquor and leave both fish and liquor to cool. If the quiche is to be cooked at once, turn up the oven to 190°C, 375°F, Gas Mark 5.

**3.** Beat the eggs one by one into the curd cheese. Grate the Parmesan if necessary and stir in with the cream. Add the fish liquor and season with pepper but no salt.

**4.** Line the tart dish with the pastry and arrange the leeks and haddock in the bottom. Do not pour in the egg and cheese mixture until just before cooking: if the quiche is to be kept, put the base with the leek and haddock and the bowl with the egg mixture (both covered) into the refrigerator. Bake for 30-35 minutes or until golden brown and just set. Eat hot or cold.

# ▪ MUSHROOM PIE WITH ▪ TUNA FISH

The amalgamation of flavours in this pie means that it will appeal to those who are bored with (or were never keen on) tuna fish. Use large mushrooms, if possible, as these have the best flavour. *For 4-6.*

PASTRY

# • INGREDIENTS •

| | |
|---|---|
| 1 lb/500 g mushrooms | Salt and pepper |
| 4 sticks celery | 7 oz/200 g tin tuna fish in brine |
| Small handful parsley (enough to make 2 tablespoons when chopped) | Juice of ½ a lemon |
| 2-3 cloves garlic | **8½ inch/22 cm tart dish** |
| Double quantity Flaky Pastry made with cream dough | |

# • METHOD •

**1** Cut off the bottoms of the stems and peel and wipe (or wash button) mushrooms; quarter if very big but otherwise leave whole. Trim the leaf end and scrape off any brownish patches on the celery; wash and finely chop. Wash, shake dry, and finely chop the parsley; peel and chop the garlic. Set the oven to 180°C, 350°F, Gas Mark 4.

**2** Line a pie dish with just over half the pastry. Arrange a layer of mushrooms in the bottom, season with pepper and (since the fish is salty) very little salt, and spread with about the same proportion of fish, celery, garlic, and parsley. Sprinkle with lemon juice and repeat until all the ingredients are used.

**3** Roll out the rest of the pastry, wet the edges of the lining, and put on the top. Press the edges together, trim, keeping the trimmings for decoration, press the pastry with a fork, and make an air-hole in the middle. Re-roll the trimmings and cut out pastry leaves or other shapes, and arrange round the hole, dampening both surfaces to make them stick. Bake for 30 minutes; cover loosely with cooking foil to prevent the pastry from becoming too coloured, and bake for a further 30 minutes.

# · RICE ·

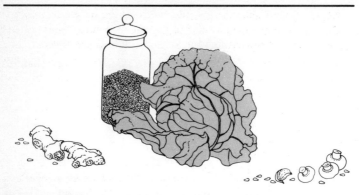

THERE are two main types of rice, long- and short-grain: long-grain is suitable for kedgeree and pilaff and to accompany stir-fries, curries, and other meat or vegetable dishes, while short-grain, which releases more starch as it cooks, is used mainly for risotto and puddings. Many kinds of each type are grown, but of the first, Patna (Indian), American long-grain, and Basmati (also Indian) are most widely available — Basmati being an especially slender-grained variety with a distinctive nutty taste which is about a third again as expensive as the former: it is, however, well worth it on occasion (at the time of writing, American long-grain is 65p per lb in Sainsbury; Basmati 93p). Risotto is made with Italian rice, which has a relatively short grain and frees enough starch to produce a slightly creamy sauce; pudding rice, which yields more, has an almost round grain (don't worry: no recipes for rice pudding have been included here). All but pudding rice can be bought brown or white; brown is nutritionally preferable and has a better flavour, but takes longer to cook.

## · SIMMERED RICE ·

Just as there are many varieties of rice, so methods of cooking it vary: the simplest, and also healthiest because none of its vitamins are poured away with the cooking liquor, is to simmer it in just as much liquid as it will absorb. I owe my introduction to this method to an excellent book called *Malaysian Cookery* by Rafi Fernandez, who also points out its advantage in health terms. A little adjustment may be needed because the absorbency of rice differs slightly, but the result will be dry and separate-grained without entailing draining, washing after cooking, and reheating, as is necessary when more liquid is used and the rice boiled in the same manner as pasta. *For 4.*

## ▪ INGREDIENTS ▪

| | |
|---|---|
| 1 lb/500 g long-grain brown rice *(the amount needed depends on appetites)* | *Salt* |
| | **Largish saucepan, preferably with a lid** |
| 1½ pints/900 ml stock or water plus a few drops of oil if water is used | |

## ▪ METHOD ▪

**1** Rinse the rice in cold water to remove surplus starch (shake it under the tap in a sieve). Put all the ingredients into the saucepan and bring to the boil. Reduce the heat, cover, and simmer for 20 minutes. Check that there is still moisture in the pan, add a little stock or water if necessary, and simmer for a further 10 minutes or until the rice is tender. Test by breaking a few grains in the fingers or tasting. Basmati should take just 30 minutes and American long-grain 30-35 (in comparison to only 18 for white of both varieties). If any liquid is left in the pan, raise the heat to moderate until it has evaporated. The rice is now ready but if kept covered will remain hot for some minutes.

# ▪ CHICKEN RISOTTO ▪

Apart from rice plus chicken stock and meat from the carcass, this demands only onion(s), parsley, Parmesan cheese, 1 oz/25 g of streaky bacon and a stick of celery per person. A little cream adds richness to the flavour but is not essential.

As risotto is meant to be moist rather than dry, with a sufficient residue of cooking-liquor for sauce, a higher proportion of liquid is given than for long-grain rice.

The stock should be made when the chicken is cut up (see page 28) but can be kept for 2 days in the refrigerator. The carcass from a previously roasted chicken can be used but will give less distinctive flavour; the risotto will also be relatively uninteresting (although still very pleasant) with less than the minimum quantity of chicken meat. *For 4.*

## ▪ INGREDIENTS ▪

| | |
|---|---|
| 1 *large or 2 medium onions* | *Salt and pepper* |
| *4 sticks celery* | *1 lb/500 g brown Italian rice* |
| *4-5 parsley leaves* | *2 tablespoons grated Parmesan cheese plus more for serving* |
| *4 oz/125 g streaky bacon* | |
| *2 pints/1.2 litres Chicken Stock (see page 28), plus the liver if available and 4-8 oz/125-250 g cooked chicken meat* | *4 tablespoons double cream (optional)* |
| | **Largish saucepan, preferably with a lid** |
| *2 tablespoons oil, if necessary* | |

## ▪ METHOD ▪

**1** Peel and chop the onion(s). Cut off the leaves and trim the root ends of the celery, wash, then dice or slice finely. Wash the parsley and leave to drain. Remove the rind from the bacon and dice the bacon, using scissors.

**2** Skim the solidified fat from the top of the stock and put about 1 oz/25 g into the saucepan; if there is not enough, supplement it with up to 2 tablespoons of oil. Fry the onion and bacon gently for 15 minutes or until colour just changes, turning frequently.

**3** Add the celery and fry for about 2 minutes. Add the stock with a little salt and rather more pepper and the rice. Bring to the boil, reduce the heat, cover and simmer for 30 minutes.

**4** Dice the chicken liver and meat, discarding any skin and fat. Finely chop the parsley. Stir the chicken into the risotto. Check that the pan is not dry (tilt slightly) and pour in a little more stock or water if necessary, then simmer for 5 more minutes. Test the rice (break a few grains between the fingers or taste). If much liquid is left in the pan, turn up the heat to moderate until only a little is left. Stir in the Parmesan, cream if it is being used, and parsley. Serve with more Parmesan.

# · CHICKEN PILAFF ·

This is less economic than risotto but more convenient, since it can be made in advance and reheated.

The pilaff will not stand as a dish on its own without a fair proportion of chicken meat (although without meat it makes an excellent accompaniment to Chicken with Orange and Brandy (see page 156) or vegetables such as broccoli or spinach). *For 4-5.*

## · INGREDIENTS ·

| | |
|---|---|
| 1½ pints/900 ml Chicken Stock (see page 28), plus the liver if available and 8 oz/250 g cooked chicken meat | 8 oz/250 g mushrooms |
| | 1 heaped teaspoon coriander seeds |
| Up to 3 tablespoons oil, if necessary | 1 level teaspoon ground cumin |
| 1 lb/500 g brown American long-grain, Patna or Basmati rice | 3½ oz/100 g almonds (preferably whole) |
| Salt and pepper | 2oz/50g raisins |
| 1 large onion | **Largish saucepan with a lid** |
| 3 cloves garlic | **Ovenware dish with a lid for reheating if made in advance** |
| 1 red pepper | |

## · METHOD ·

**1** Skim the fat from the top of the stock and put about 1½ oz/40 g into a frying pan; if there is not enough, supplement it with up to 3 tablespoons oil. Set aside.
**2** Rinse the rice under the cold tap and put into the saucepan with the stock and a little salt and pepper. Bring to the boil,

lower the heat, cover, and simmer for 20 minutes. Check that it is not dry, then simmer for a further 10 minutes or until it is tender (taste or break between the fingers).

**3** While the rice simmers, peel and finely chop the onion and garlic; wash and quarter the pepper, discarding the core, seeds, and inner flesh, then chop into small squares or short lengths. Trim the mushroom stalks, wash small mushrooms or peel and wipe large ones, and slice.

**4** Fry the onion in the chicken fat for 7-10 minutes or until soft; add the garlic, mushrooms, pepper and spices. Slightly increase the heat, and fry for 5 minutes more or until the mushrooms exude juice and are soft. Add the almonds, raisins, and chicken meat and liver, toss to coat in the oil, and if the rice is tender (or the pilaff being made in advance) fry for 2-3 minutes; if not, remove from the heat and wait until the rice is ready to continue frying. Gently mix the fried ingredients with the rice and serve. If made in advance, turn into the ovenware dish, cover, and reheat 20-30 minutes at 180°C, 350°F, Gas Mark 4.

# · Stir-Fried Vegetables ·

Stir-frying has become so popular that it probably needs little introduction. I was first induced to try it by Yan-kit So in the *Wok Cookbook*, on whose clear instructions the technique described below is based. It is a wonderfully easy and effective way of turning ingredients which might otherwise be bland into a dish with zest and interest. In part, this is achieved by flavourings, notably soy, but very quick cooking, which especially suits vegetables because they retain their original crispness, also contributes — and has the additional advantage of causing minimum loss of nutrients.

Its most obvious disadvantage is that all the ingredients have to be diced, although this often does not take much longer than the chopping and slicing needed for other methods of cookery; I should also point out, however, that, despite the fact that the oil required is light (and also relatively cheap), one cannot avoid using a substantial amount, which means that the result is by no means low-calorie.

The basic technique is to chop all the ingredients into small pieces and fry for a matter of minutes over high heat, stirring continuously to ensure even cooking. Non-liquid flavourings such as ginger are put into the pan first so that the flavour is imparted to the oil; items are then added in order of cooking time and soy sauce stirred in right at the very end. Rice can be served separately so that the ingredients act as a sauce, or fried with them as part of the dish (another alternative is pasta or noodles: see page 29).

Most vegetables can be cooked in this way: those which cannot include peas and beans (out of their pods), sea-kale beet (as opposed to spinach), and, rather obviously, tomatoes. Most also take 2-3 minutes to fry but some, such as aubergines, peppers, cabbage, cauliflower and broccoli, take longer: the last three are more successful if boiled briefly before frying (cabbage fried long enough to be tender without boiling tends to burn). Two which cook relatively quickly (1-2 minutes) are spinach and mushrooms. For a meal, a selection of 3 or 4 will make an attractively varied dish. The choice can be governed by prices and preference, but bear in mind that (as with salads) texture and colour play their part as well as flavour; it is also a good idea to step up the protein content of the meal by adding nuts or seeds or including relatively protein-rich vegetables, notably spinach or bean-sprouts.

The recipes below are intended merely as examples: others can be composed from the list of stir-frying times given on page 57; for a table of nutritional values, see page 189.

Except aubergines and courgettes and those which need boiling, it is preferable not to cut up vegetables far in advance, partly because it causes loss of vitamin C; also, they may dry out or wilt and lose their crispness.

Use natural soy, i.e. shoyu or tamari, rather than soy sauce with additives.

The ginger must be fresh root as opposed to preserved or ground: if root is not available, it is best to omit it altogether, as any substitute will produce an unsatisfactory result.

Quantities are for 2-3 because this amount can comfortably be fried in an average-width large saucepan (a frying pan is really too shallow to allow you to both hold the ingredients and also stir them easily).

# · STIR-FRIED BROCCOLI ·
# WITH BEAN-SPROUTS

The difference between large and button mushrooms is very noticeable in a stir-fry: either may seem preferable according to the other ingredients, but for this recipe the firmness of button ones works better.

Spring rather than large onions are usually used to flavour the oil for stir-fried and other dishes of Eastern origin.

## · INGREDIENTS ·

| | |
|---|---|
| 8 oz/250 g broccoli | ½ red pepper |
| Salt | 1-2 spring onions |
| 4 oz/125 g bean-sprouts | ⅓ inch/1 cm slice root ginger |
| 8 oz/250 g brown or white American long-grain, Patna or Basmati rice | 2 teaspoons soy sauce |
| | 3 tablespoons sunflower oil |
| ¾ pint/450 ml water plus a few drops of oil | **Saucepan with a lid** |
| | **Large saucepan (or wok)** |
| 4 oz/125 g button mushrooms | |

## · METHOD ·

**1** Wash the broccoli and chop into pieces with stalks about ¼ inch/0.75 cm thick, florets about ½ inch/1.5 cm across, and 1-1½ inches/3-4 cm long. Set a pan of water to boil (if it is quicker, boil a kettle). Add the broccoli with a little salt, bring back to the boil, and boil for 2 minutes. Drain immediately and refresh under the cold tap. Leave to drain in a colander (it is important that items should be dry when they are fried or the oil will spit).

**2** Pick over the bean-sprouts, removing any rotten ones; wash and leave to dry with the broccoli.

**3** Rinse the rice. Put into the saucepan with a lid, add the water and drops of oil, season with a little salt, and bring to the boil.

Lower the heat and simmer, covered, for 18 minutes or until tender if white, 30-35 minutes if brown. When cooked, leave to keep hot with the lid on the pan; do not start frying the vegetables until it is ready.

**4** While the rice cooks, prepare the other vegetables. Trim the stalks of the mushrooms, wash, dry with kitchen roll, and chop into slices about ¼ inch/0.75 cm thick. Wash, dry, and quarter the pepper; remove the white inner flesh and any seeds or dark spots and cut into strips about ¼ inch/0.75 cm wide and 1 inch/2.5 cm long. Cut the root and green leaves from the onions, peel, and cut into thickish slices; peel, wipe if necessary, and thinly slice the ginger.

**5** Set all the prepared ingredients and the soy sauce to hand. Heat the oil for a few moments over high heat in the large saucepan. Add the ginger, wait a few moments, then add the onion (do not stir yet). Allow to fry until just beginning to brown, when the smell of the ginger especially will suddeny become very perceptible. Add the pepper and start stirring: stir continuously for 1-1½ minutes, until the skin is slightly seared. Add the sprouts and broccoli and continue to stir for another minute. Add the mushrooms and stir for a further 1-2 minutes (at this stage, one can see when the vegetables are ready: stop at once if the broccoli starts looking ragged or disintegrating). Stir in the soy and remove from the heat. Serve piled on top of the rice.

# STIR-FRIED CABBAGE AND · AUBERGINE WITH TOASTED · SUNFLOWER SEEDS

Red pepper adds colour. The aubergine must sweat for an hour.

## · INGREDIENTS ·

| | |
|---|---|
| 1 *medium aubergine, weighing about 8 oz/250 g* | *Salt, some of which should be finely ground* |

| | |
|---|---|
| *About 8 oz/250 g (½ small) cabbage* | *4 oz/125 g dwarf, Kenya or other non-string beans* |
| *8 oz/250 g brown or white American long-grain, Patna or Basmati rice* | *4 cloves garlic* |
| | *2 teaspoons soy sauce* |
| *¾ pint/450 ml water plus a few drops of oil* | *4 tablespoons sunflower oil* |
| | **Saucepan with a lid** |
| *1 oz/25 g sunflower seeds* | **Large saucepan** |
| *½ red pepper* | **Small saucepan** |

## • METHOD •

**1** Wash and chop the aubergine into ⅓ inch/1 cm squares. For quick chopping, cut into slices 1 cm thick, pile 3 or 4 slices on top of each other, and cross-cut. Sprinkle with fine salt and allow to sweat for 1 hour in a colander. Rinse and leave to drain.

**2** Halve the cabbage lengthwise; remove the outermost leaves if damaged and similarly slice and cut into ⅓ inch/1 cm squares, discarding the stalk. Bring a pan of slightly salted water to the boil; put in the cabbage, return to the boil and boil for 2 minutes. Rinse in cold water and leave to drain in a sieve (do not add to the aubergine).

**3** Rinse the rice. Put into the saucepan with a lid, add the water and drops of oil, season with a little salt, and bring to the boil. Lower the heat and simmer, covered, for 18 minutes or until tender if white, 30-35 minutes if brown.

**4** Toast the sunflower seeds. Put into a small saucepan; do not add oil but simply set over fairly high heat and shake often so that they heat evenly: after 2-3 minutes they will start to turn golden and smell rather like roasted hazelnuts. Continue to hold over the heat but shake constantly for about another minute, until they have coloured evenly.

**5** Wash, dry, and quarter the pepper; remove the white inner flesh and any seeds or dark spots and cut into strips about ¼ inch/0.75 cm wide and 1 inch/2.5 cm long. Wash, top and tail, and slice the beans into 1-1½ inch/3-4 cm strips; dry by laying on a plate lined with kitchen roll and blot with more kitchen roll. Peel and finely slice the garlic.

**6** Put all the prepared ingredients and the soy within reach. Blot the aubergine and cabbage with kitchen roll if they are still damp. Heat the oil for a moment or two in the large saucepan; add the garlic and allow to fry without stirring until it is just starting to change colour. Add the aubergine and pepper and stir for 1½ minutes; put in the beans and stir for another minute; add the cabbage and stir for 1-2 minutes. Add and stir in the seeds and soy. Remove from the heat and serve with the rice.

# · STIR-FRIED COURGETTES · AND SPINACH WITH RICE AND CASHEW NUTS

If the rice is to be stirred into the vegetables, more soy is needed than in the previous two recipes.

If so-called spinach has very large leaves and thick white stalks, it is not real spinach but sea-kale beet, which, though an acceptable alternative for most purposes, is unsuitable for stir-frying, since the leaves collapse in tatters as soon as they are cooked (the stalks can be stir-fried and have a slightly spinach-like taste but are only worth using with quantities of 8 oz/250 g or more. To prepare sea-kale beet, first strip off the tough outer casing on larger stems and then chop as given in the directions above for non-string beans; remember to fry it for 1 minute longer than you would spinach).

## · INGREDIENTS ·

| | |
|---|---|
| About 8 oz/250 g courgettes | 8 oz/250 g brown American long-grain, Patna or Basmati rice |
| Salt, some of which should be finely ground | ¾ pint/450 ml water plus a few drops of oil |
| About 8 oz/250 g (½ small) cauliflower | |
| | 4 oz/125 g large mushrooms |
| 4 oz/125 g spinach | 2-3 cloves garlic |

| | |
|---|---|
| ⅓ inch/1 cm square piece root ginger | 1 tablespoon soy sauce |
| 2 oz/50 g cashew nuts or pieces | **Saucepan with lid** |
| 4 tablespoons sunflower oil | **Large saucepan** |

## ▪ METHOD ▪

**1** Wash the courgettes, scrape off damaged or brownish surfaces, and cut into matchsticks ¼ inch/0.75 cm wide and 1 inch/2.5 cm long (for quick cutting, slice at 1-inch intervals, stand the slices on end, and cross-chop: this method is also suitable for carrots). Put into a colander, sprinkle with finely ground salt, and leave for 1 hour to sweat. Rinse and drain.

**2** Divide the cauliflower lengthwise; store the part not needed in a bag in the refrigerator. Cut into pieces, with stalks ¼ inch/0.75 cm thick, florets ½ inch/1.5 cm across, and 1-1½ inches/3-4 cm long. Bring to the boil in a pan of salted water, boil for 2 minutes, then rinse, and leave to drain in a sieve (do not put into the colander with the courgettes).

**3** Wash the spinach and leave to drain (if necessary on top of the cauliflower).

**4** Rinse the rice. Put into a saucepan with a lid, add the water and drops of oil, season with a little salt, and bring to the boil. Lower the heat and simmer, covered, for 18 minutes or until tender if white, 30-35 minutes if brown.

**5** Trim the stalks of the mushrooms; peel, wipe, and cut into ⅓ inch/1 cm squares. Peel and slice the garlic; peel the ginger, wipe if necessary, and slice thinly. Roughly chop the nuts.

**6** Cut the spinach into strips about ½ inch/1.5 cm thick; place on a plate lined with kitchen roll and blot to absorb any remaining moisture. If necessary, blot the cauliflower and courgettes. Loosen the rice round the edges of the saucepan and stir gently. Set all the prepared ingredients to hand. Heat the oil for a moment or two and put in the garlic and ginger; allow to fry until slightly coloured. Add the cauliflower, courgettes, and nuts and stir for 1 minute; put in the mushrooms and spinach and stir for 1-2 minutes until the mushrooms are soft. Add the rice as quickly as possible, stir to mix, and add the soy; stir again and remove from the heat.

## • Vegetable Stir-Frying Times •

Aubergine: 3½-5 minutes
Beans (stringless): 2-3 minutes
Bean sprouts: 2-3 minutes
Broccoli: boil 2 minutes, stir-fry 2-3 minutes
Cabbage: boil 2 minutes, stir-fry 1-2 minutes
Carrots: 2-3 minutes
Cauliflower: boil 2 minutes; stir-fry 2-3 minutes
Celeriac: 2-3 minutes
Celery: 2-3 minutes

Chilli (green): 4-5 minutes
Courgettes: 2-3 minutes
Fennel: 2-3 minutes
Leeks: 2-3 minutes
Mushrooms: 1-2 minutes
Onions: 2-3 minutes
Parsnip: 2-3 minutes
Pepper (green): 3-4 minutes
Pepper (red): 3½-5 minutes
Sea-kale beet stems: 2-3 minutes
Spinach: 1-2 minutes
Turnip: 2-3 minutes

The following are unsuitable for stir-frying: **Broad beans, Peas, Potatoes, Red cabbage, Sea-kale beet leaves, Sweetcorn, Tomatoes.**

# • KEDGEREE •

LIKE curry, this originated in India, though it has long been accepted as a traditional British and in particular breakfast dish.

Either all of it (except parsley) or just the fish and eggs can be prepared in advance.

As with other dishes made with fish and despite the fact that the rice can be boiled in the fish water, it has far more flavour if the haddock is baked rather than boiled; flavour is also the reason why butter is recommended instead of oil (those who prefer not to use so much, however, could substitute oil for frying the onion). *For* 4.

## • INGREDIENTS •

| | |
|---|---|
| 8 oz/250 g brown American long-grain, Patna or Basmati rice | ¾ pint/450 ml water plus a few drops of oil |

Salt and pepper

| | |
|---|---|
| 1½ lb/750 g smoked haddock | 4 or 5 parsley leaves or 1 teaspoon nutmeg |
| 2½-2¾ oz/65-70 g unsalted or lightly salted butter | **Saucepan preferably with lid** |
| 4 eggs, preferably large | **Ovenware dish** |
| 1 large or 2 medium onions | |

## • METHOD •

**1** Set the oven to 200°C, 400°F, Gas Mark 6. Rinse the rice in a sieve under the cold tap and put into the saucepan with the water, a little salt, and the oil. Bring to the boil, reduce the heat to a simmer, cover, and cook for 20 minutes; check that the pan is not dry, and continue simmering 10 minutes or until tender.

**2** While it cooks, rinse the fish in cold water and skin if necessary; pull sharply from one corner and ease off any skin which sticks with a knife. Lay the flesh on a piece of cooking foil large enough to wrap it into a parcel, season with pepper (no salt), and dot with about 1 oz/25 g of the butter. Wrap, place on a baking dish, and bake 20 minutes or until it flakes when prodded with a fork. If the kedgeree is for immediate consumption, turn down the oven to 180°C, 350°F, Gas Mark 4.

**3** Meanwhile, put the eggs in a saucepan with enough water to cover, bring to the boil and boil for 12 minutes; leave to cool. Peel and finely chop the onion; fry gently in another 1 oz/25 g of the butter, turning often, for 15 minutes or until just beginning to turn brown.

**4.** Flake the fish into smallish pieces, removing all bones; peel and chop the eggs. Put into the ovenware dish with the rice and onion; season generously with pepper, add the nutmeg if using instead of parsley, and mix. Dot the top with the remaining ½-¾ oz/15-20 g butter and heat for 15-20 minutes. Wash, drain, and finely chop parsley, if it is being used, and stir in just before serving.

# · STIR-FRIED SWEET AND ·
# SOUR PORK

Few dishes are simpler or quicker to prepare — but success depends on marinating the meat for at least an hour and drying it thoroughly before frying.

To balance the richness of the sauce, I suggest serving with fresh-tasting crudités such as cucumber, celery, green pepper, or crisp raw cauliflower florets.

Sherry makes quite a difference. Without it, you may prefer to reverse the proportions of vinegar to soy: use 4 tablespoons of soy, 2 of vinegar and, to replace the sherry, 4 of water. *For 4.*

## · INGREDIENTS ·

| | |
|---|---|
| *4 pork chops* | *12 oz/375 g brown or white American long-grain, Patna or Basmati rice* |
| *4 oz/125 g soft brown sugar* | |
| *2 teaspoons cornflour* | *1⅛ pints/680 ml water* |
| *4 tablespoons wine vinegar* | *⅓ inch/1 cm square slice root ginger* |
| *2 tablespoons soy sauce* | |
| *4 tablespoons dry sherry or water* | *2 cloves garlic* |
| *Salt* | **Saucepan with a lid** |
| *4 tablespoons sunflower oil* | **Sharp knife** |

## · METHOD ·

**1** Wash the chops and cut away the bone and outside fat. Slice the main part of the meat lengthwise into strips ¼ inch/0.75 cm wide, and chop into sticks about 1 inch/2.5 cm long (this will give a tenderer result than cutting into sticks across). Cut the end part of the chops whichever way seems most practicable.

**2** Mix together the sugar, cornflour, vinegar, soy, sherry or water, ½ level teaspoon salt and 2 tablespoons of the oil. Pour over the meat and leave to marinate.

**3** Rinse the rice, bring to the boil in the water with a pinch of salt and a little oil, then simmer, covered, for 18 minutes or until tender for white rice or 30-35 minutes for brown. Leave in the saucepan with the lid on to keep hot; wait until it is cooked before frying the pork.

**4** Peel the ginger and garlic, wiping the ginger if necessary, then slice both fairly thinly. Dry the pork; wrap and squeeze a few strips at a time in kitchen roll and place on a plate lined with kitchen roll (this is messy, but if omitted the oil will spit when the meat is put into the pan and beads of sauce may burn as it fries).

**5** If cooking with gas (which is immediately adjustable), heat the oil over medium to high heat; with electricity, use high heat but lift the pan to cool it a little before adding the meat. Put in the ginger and garlic and allow to brown slightly. Add the meat, raise the heat on a gas ring, and stir for 2 minutes. Pour in the marinade and cook at high heat, stirring every now and again, for 5 minutes or until the sauce is dark and reduced. Serve at once.

# VEGETABLE
# ·AND EGG DISHES·

THIS CHAPTER was planned with Shirley Conran's 'Life is too short to stuff a mushroom' in mind — so, although (to be literal) stuffed dishes are included (one with mushroom stuffing rather than vice versa), this chapter contains nothing very fussy or which takes a long time to prepare. The only recipe which might have been given here and does in fact take a little longer is Steve's Moussaka, which I have put in the chapter on parties. At the other extreme, very quick egg dishes, such as omelettes, have been omitted because everyone should already know how to make them.

# · RATATOUILLE ·

This is a Provençal dish in which vegetables are stewed very slowly in their own juices. Since it contains vegetables only, it is not usually served alone except as a first course. However, it can make an excellent main course, hot or cold, provided that lack of protein is compensated for at other meals or by serving it with Cheese Bread (see page 114).

Choose firm aubergines and peppers and, if possible, small courgettes which will have more bite.

Remember to allow an hour for the aubergines to sweat before starting the recipe. *For 4.*

## ▪ INGREDIENTS ▪

| | |
|---|---|
| 1 *large or 2 smallish aubergines, weighing 1-1¼ lb/500-625 g* | 12 *oz/375 g courgettes* |
| *Salt, including some finely ground* | 1 *tablespoon oil, preferably olive* |
| | *Pepper* |
| 3 *cloves garlic* | 1 *lb/500 g ripe tomatoes* |
| 1 *large or 2 medium onions* | **Large saucepan with lid or a flameproof casserole (one which can be put over heat)** |
| 2 *peppers, preferably including 1 red* | |

## ▪ METHOD ▪

**1** Wash and cut the aubergine(s) into slices about ⅓ inch/1 cm thick, sprinkle each slice with a little fine salt, and put into a colander for 1 hour to sweat. Rinse under the tap and shake off surplus moisture.

**2** Peel and finely chop the garlic and onion(s); wash, quarter, and slice the peppers into strips, removing the seeds, white inner flesh, and any dark spots from a red one; wash the courgettes, peel off any damaged or discoloured surfaces, and slice a little more thickly than the aubergines (sweating and salting the courgettes is unnecessary in this recipe, where a certain amount of vegetable juice is needed).

**3** Cover the bottom of the saucepan or casserole with the oil and fry the onion over low heat, turning often, for 10 minutes or until soft but not brown. Add the garlic and continue frying for 5 more minutes. Add the aubergine, peppers, and courgettes, season very lightly with salt and a little more generously with pepper. Mix gently, put on the lid, and reduce the heat to the lowest possible. Stew gently for 45 minutes, turning the vegetables carefully once or twice during that time. The vegetables will cook in the steam and there will be juice collecting in the bottom of the pan.

**4** Peel, chop, and add the tomatoes. Season again, turn up the heat slightly, replace the lid, and stew for 15 minutes. Turn the vegetables carefully to avoid breaking them, and continue stewing for a further 15-20 minutes, until they are soft but not so that they are disintegrating.

# · AUBERGINE BAKED WITH · MOZZARELLA

To achieve the sticky, melting cheese top which is part of the character of the dish, the cheese really has to be mozzarella.

As mozzarella is meant to be moist, it is generally packaged in whey (which needs to be drained off before use): sometimes, however, it is sold ready grated, which makes it go further but somewhat spoils the point of it, since once it becomes dry it loses its special quality.

Allow an hour for the aubergines to sweat. *For 3-4.*

## · INGREDIENTS ·

| | |
|---|---|
| 2 aubergines, weighing 1¼-1½ lb/ 625-750 g | ½ teaspoon dried oregano |
| 1 large onion | 1 tablespoon tomato paste |
| 3-4 tablespoons oil | ⅛ pint/80 ml water |
| Small handful parsley | 8 oz/250 g mozzarella |
| 3 cloves garlic | **Large baking tray** |
| 1½ lb/750 g ripe tomatoes | **Shallow ovenware dish** |
| Salt and pepper | |

## · METHOD ·

**1** Wash and chop the aubergines into ⅓ inch/1 cm slices. Sprinkle with fine salt and leave in a colander for 1 hour to sweat. Rinse, shake off surplus moisture, and blot dry on a plate lined with kitchen roll.

**2** Line the baking tray with cooking foil: if the tray has no sides which will prevent oil dripping off, turn up the edges of the foil. Spread with 1-1½ tablespoons of oil and place as many slices on it as will fit without overlapping (a 12 inch/30 cm tray will take just over half). Turn the slices over to coat with oil on both sides, set the grill to medium, and grill for 5-7 minutes until pale brown or mottled with brown (the slices tend to colour more in the middle). Transfer to a plate, spread the foil with another tablespoon of oil, and grill the rest.

**3** Wash the parsley and leave to drain. Peel and finely chop the onion and garlic; peel and chop the tomatoes, discarding cores.

**4** Fry the onion over low heat in 1 tablespoon of oil for 10 minutes or until soft, turning frequently. Add the garlic and fry for another 5 minutes. Stir in the tomatoes, season with salt and pepper. Sprinkle with the oregano, then simmer for 10 minutes. Dissolve the tomato paste in the water, add, and continue simmering for 5 more minutes or until the sauce has thickened slightly. Remove from the heat. Finely chop and add the parsley.

**5.** While the sauce simmers, set the oven to 200°C, 400°F, Gas Mark 6. Arrange the aubergine in the bottom of the ovenware dish; spread with sauce, drain and slice the mozzarella, and arrange on top. Bake for 15 minutes or until the cheese is golden and bubbling.

# · STUFFED MARROW ·

The great merit of marrows is their cheapness. They make a splendid-looking meal cooked whole, but can be sliced if you haven't got a dish large enough for a whole one.

The base for the filling can be curd or other medium-fat soft cheese, or yoghurt and/or cream. Using just cream is consistent with neither health, nor the economy represented by the marrow, but has the advantages of flavour and that the top will brown in the oven. Yoghurt will not brown but Greek or Greek-style is an excellent substitute for cream in terms of flavour.

Initial baking rather than boiling is recommended to reduce wateriness. Altogether, baking takes nearly 1½ hours. *For* 4.

## · INGREDIENTS ·

| | |
|---|---|
| *3½-4 lb/1.75-2 kg marrow* | *2 oz/50 g walnuts or walnut pieces* |
| *2 medium onions* | *About 2 tablespoons oil* |

| | |
|---|---|
| 8 oz/250 g mushrooms (large ones tend to have more flavour than small but button ones provide a desirable contrast to the softness of the marrow) | 8 oz/250 g curd cheese plus 6 tablespoons milk; or ¼ pint/ 150 ml double cream; or ½ pint/ 300 ml yoghurt, preferably Greek, plus 2 teaspoons flour; or ¼ pint/150 ml yoghurt plus 1 teaspoon flour and ¼ pint/150 ml double cream |
| 1 large or 2 small Bramley or similar cooking apples, weighing about 12 oz/375 g | |
| Salt and pepper | **Very large ovenware dish or a baking sheet** |
| ¼ pint/150 ml water | |

## · METHOD ·

**1** Set the oven to 150°C, 300°F, Gas Mark 2. Wash the marrow and bake for 1 hour, either whole or in slices large enough for a portion, i.e. 1½-2 inches/4-5 cms thick. If no sufficiently large dish is available, use a baking sheet covered with 2 layers of cooking foil turned up at the edges like a dish. When cooked, leave until cool enough to handle, slice a whole marrow length-wise, scoop out the soft, fibrous centre and all the pips, and turn upside down to drain; with slices, simply remove the centres (they will practically fall out). Leave the oven on.

**2** Peel and slice the onions; trim the stalks of the mushrooms, wash button or peel and wipe large ones, and slice finely; quarter, core, peel, and slice the apples; roughly chop the walnuts.

**3** Fry the onions gently in the oil for 10 minutes, turning frequently. Add the mushrooms, season moderately with salt and pepper, and fry for 5-7 minutes more or until the onions are changing colour. Stir in the apple, add the water, and turn up the heat. Cook over high heat for 4-5 minutes until the apple is soft and the liquid reduced to about 2 tablespoons. Stir in the walnuts and remove from the heat.

**4** Turn the oven to 180°C, 350°F, Gas Mark 4. Blend the cheese with the milk or cream, or the yoghurt with cream, and mix with the fried ingredients. Put the marrow halves or slices back into the baking dish, season very lightly, and stuff with the mixture. Bake for 25 minutes, or (with cream) until the top of the stuffing is just beginning to brown.

# Pancakes with
# · Mushroom Stuffing ·

Although fried, pancakes need surprisingly little oil — less than a tablespoon for cooking four average servings.

If possible, make the batter an hour or so in advance. This gives the starch time to swell, which thickens the batter and produces a smoother result.

The mushroom stuffing given here is only one of many possibilities: others are Spinach (see page 70) and Leek (see page 161).

White, brown, or a mixture of flours can be used, but pancakes made with all wholemeal are much more interesting; also, the batter is easier to mix, since white flour tends to form lumps when combined with liquid. *For 8 smallish pancakes.*

## · INGREDIENTS ·

| | |
|---|---|
| *2 eggs, size 2* | *Salt and pepper* |
| *1 teaspoon of oil plus a little more for frying* | *½ pint/300 ml milk plus a little extra, if necessary* |
| *4 oz/125 g plain flour* | |

### MUSHROOM STUFFING

| | |
|---|---|
| *Small bunch parsley (enough to make 2 tablespoons when chopped) or a few stems dill* | *½ oz/15 g butter plus 1 tablespoon oil, or 2 tablespoons oil* |
| *1 lb/500 g mushrooms, preferably large* | *1 oz/25 g flour (preferably white)* |
| *3 cloves garlic* | *2 teaspoons French mustard (e.g. Grey Poupon)* |
| *½ pint/300 ml milk* | |

| As a smooth surface prevents the batter from sticking, a non-stick frying pan is an advantage | Fish slice |
| --- | --- |
| | Largish shallow ovenproof dish |

## • METHOD •

**1** To make the batter, break the eggs into a small bowl, add a teaspoon of oil, and beat smooth with a fork. Mix the flour with a generous pinch of salt and pepper. Make a well in the centre and pour in the eggs. Stir, moving outwards until all the flour is incorporated.

**2** Add the ½ pint/300 ml milk by degrees, stirring continuously. (If white flour forms lumps, press them out on the side of the bowl.) Leave to stand.

**3** Meanwhile, make the filling. Wash the herbs, shake or blot dry on kitchen roll, remove the central stem from dill, and finely chop. Cut off the bottoms of the stems and peel and wipe the mushrooms (or wash button ones); chop into even slices. Peel and finely chop the garlic.

**4** Heat but do not boil the milk. Fry the mushrooms and garlic in the butter and/or oil over very gentle heat for 10-15 minutes until the mushrooms have exuded juice and are soft but not brown. Season moderately with salt and pepper, stir in the flour, then add the milk, stirring continuously until the sauce is thick. Stir in the mustard and herbs.

**5** Set the oven to 200°C, 400°F, Gas Mark 6.

**6** Stir the batter thoroughly; if it seems very thick, add a little extra milk.

**7** Turn the ring to about two-thirds of its hottest heat. Spread a very little oil over the bottom of the frying pan: with a small pan, a teaspoonful is enough, or you can simply moisten the surface with a pastry brush or oiled kitchen roll. Set the pan on the heat and as soon as the oil starts to smoke add less batter than reaches the sides of the pan. Tilt quickly to spread it to the edges: this ensures a thin pancake. The batter takes only moments to cook: lift it at the sides as it sets with the fish slice and turn (or toss) when it is deep gold.

**8** Spread the filling over it as the second side cooks; this may be mottled rather than smoothly coloured and is ready when either gold or freckled with brown. Roll it up and place in the ovenproof dish. Repeat to make 8 pancakes; the oil needs replacing only after every second or third pancake.

**9** When all the pancakes are fried and filled, heat in the oven for 15 minutes.

**Variation** The mushroom stuffing can be turned into fish or chicken stuffing by replacing a proportion of the mushrooms with a corresponding amount of cooked diced or flaked chicken or fish (e.g. cod, haddock, plaice, shrimps, prawns, or crab). Add to the sauce with the herbs.

# · CHEESE SOUFFLÉ ·

$A$ soufflé will rise much more dramatically than Gougère — but sinks almost as soon as it is taken from the oven, so it is essential to eat it immediately.

It is not especially filling nor does it go well with other items, so serve alone and follow with salad, such as Beans with Onions (see page 102).

Soufflés are normally baked in deep soufflé dishes with vertical sides for maximum rising, but one can get a very acceptable result with a bowl-shaped dish such as the bottom of a deep casserole (even in a pie dish, a soufflé will rise quite reasonably). An egg whisk, however, is essential. *For* 4.

## · INGREDIENTS ·

| | |
|---|---|
| ½ pint/300 ml milk | 6 oz/190 g strong Cheddar cheese |
| ½ oz/15 g butter plus 1 tablespoon oil, or 2 tablespoons oil | Slim bunch chives (enough for about 1 tablespoon when chopped), optional |
| Scant 1 oz/25 g plain flour | |
| 2 teaspoons French mustard (e.g. Grey Poupon) | 4 eggs, size 1 or 2 |
| Salt and pepper | |

68

| 8½ inch/21 cm soufflé dish or other dish of similar diameter and at least 4½ inches/11 cm deep | Egg whisk |
|---|---|
| | 2 large bowls |

## ▪ METHOD ▪

**1** Heat but do not boil the milk. Melt the butter with the oil, or warm the oil, over gentle heat. Add the flour and stir until smooth. Slowly pour in the milk, stirring continuously. Continue stirring for 3-5 minutes until the sauce thickens. Remove from the heat, stir in the mustard, and season lightly with salt and generously with pepper. Turn into one of the large bowls and leave for a few minutes to cool.

**2** Set the oven to 200°C, 400°F, Gas Mark 6. Grease the soufflé or other dish. Coarsely grate the cheese; wash the chives if they are being used and leave to drain.

**3** Separate the egg yolks and whites. Wash the eggs (in case bits of shell fall into the whites) and break each one over a cup or bowl by itself so that if any yolk escapes the rest are not affected. Crack smartly in the middle and tip the yolk from one half of the shell to the other until all the white has fallen into the cup. If a yolk breaks or drops with the white by accident and cannot be entirely removed the egg will have to be used for something else, since if yolk is present the whites will not whip satisfactorily. Empty the yolks into the sauce and transfer the whites to the second large bowl.

**4** Stir the yolks into the sauce; finely chop the chives and add with the cheese. Mix well.

**5** Add a pinch of salt to the whites (this will help to make them whisk more smoothly) and whisk until they are close-textured and stiff enough to hold their shape when twirled or dropped from the whisk.

**6** Fold (very lightly stir, almost lift) the whites into the sauce, turning the mixture over from the bottom upwards in a figure of eight until no pockets of white remain. Slide it into the soufflé dish and put it into the oven immediately. Bake for 35 minutes without opening the oven door. When ready, it will be deep brown and if cooked in a vertical-sided dish probably with a collar of yellow where the surface has broken during rising.

# · GOUGÈRE ·

Like traditional after-dinner savouries in this country, which were served as an accompaniment to (principally) port, gougère was designed to go with wine — in this case, Burgundy. It is made of choux pastry and, because of the addition of cheese, rises very evenly. As it also tends to spread, it is usually shaped into a single ring, rather than buns. If the centre is filled, serve hot: suggested fillings are Mushroom, as for pancakes (see page 66), Leek (page 161) or Spinach (below). If unfilled, serve hot or cold with a salad such as Beans with Onions or Mushroom and Pepper (see pages 102 and 97). If the vegetable sold as spinach has large leaves and thick white stems, it is in fact sea-kale beet, which is an acceptable substitute for most purposes. Cut out the stems, which can be used for stir-frying (see page 55).

White and/or wholemeal flour can be used, but as wholemeal is less absorbent than white, it does not take up quite all the fat from the proportions of butter and cheese given below; with wholemeal alone, ½ oz/15 g less cheese is recommended to counter this.

As precise measurements matter, accurate metric equivalents rather than convenient approximations are given. *For 4.*

## ▪ INGREDIENTS ▪

| | |
|---|---|
| 2½ oz/70 g white self-raising flour | 4½ oz/135 g strong Cheddar cheese |
| 2 oz/50 g wholemeal flour | |
| Salt and pepper | 3 eggs, size 3 (if using larger ones, remove a little from one of them) |
| 2 oz/60 g butter | |
| Scant ½ pint/280 ml water | |

### SPINACH FILLING (OPTIONAL)

| | |
|---|---|
| 8 oz/250 g spinach, or sea-kale beet | 1 oz/25 g Parmesan cheese |
| 3 oz/90 g ricotta or other medium-fat soft cheese | 2 tablespoons milk |

| 8-9 inch/20-22 cm tart dish or other shallow ovenware dish | Large saucepan with a lid (for the filling) |
| --- | --- |

## ▪ METHOD ▪

**1** To make the gougère, mix the flours, season lightly with salt and more generously with pepper, and put into a mug (this makes it easier to add it all at the same time).

**2** Chop up the butter, put into a smallish saucepan with the water, and heat gently until the butter has melted. Bring to the boil. As soon as bubbling is vigorous, tip in the flour, turn off the heat and beat until the mixture is perfectly smooth and very stiff; this will take several minutes. Leave the mixture to cool for a further 4 or 5 minutes.

**3.** Coarsely grate the Cheddar. Set the oven to 190°C, 375°F, Gas Mark 5. Add one egg to the dough and beat until it is completely incorporated and the mixture is again very stiff. Repeat with the second and third eggs: after the second, the dough will be softer, and after the third will have the consistency of whipped cream. Stir in the cheese.

**4** Place dollops of pastry round the edge of the baking dish and smooth into a high, continuous circle. Bake for 50 minutes; do not open the oven door during cooking. When ready, the gougère will have risen to at least double its original size and be a deep, rich brown colour.

**5** Meanwhile, make the filling. Pick over the spinach; cut out beet stalks. Wash well. Pile the spinach into the large saucepan with a sprinkling of salt and 1 tablespoon water; with beet, add about 2 inches/5-6 cm (theoretically, spinach needs no water at all, since enough is provided by the residue of washing water on the leaves and, as it starts to cook, its own juices; I suggest a tablespoonful, however, just in case). Put on the lid and set over medium heat for 6-7 minutes for spinach or until covered with juice and tender; 10-12 minutes for beet. Turn into a colander, press out surplus liquid, and chop roughly.

**6** Grate the Parmesan if necessary. Beat together the cheeses and milk, add a moderate sprinkling of pepper, and mix with the spinach or beet.

**7** Arrange in the centre of the cooked gougère and heat for 7-10 minutes at 180°C, 350°F, Gas Mark 4.

# · MEAT AND FISH ·

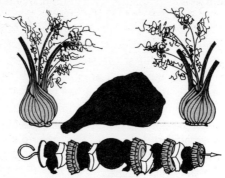

Prices have led me to give a disproportionate number of recipes in this chapter for chicken (even free-range chicken, although about 30% more expensive than battery, is still much cheaper than beef or lamb). To economize, and also because free-range poultry is not always available in portions, I have suggested buying a whole chicken or half leg of lamb and dividing it yourself, which not only reduces the initial cost but means that you can make use of the remaining meat and bones by making soups and other dishes. Obviously, you may not always have time for this (although it really does not take very long to do), but it seemed helpful at least to put forward the idea and explain how to do it.

As for fish, my original intention was to devote half, if not more, of the chapter to it: in the end, because of the expense, I have included only 2 recipes.

## · BEEFBURGERS ·

Mixing and shaping one's own beefburgers takes only a few minutes and not only gives a better-tasting result but guarantees that they contain no additives. The issue of the quality of the beef itself is another matter. Use finely minced, lean beef if possible. *For 8-10 burgers.*

## • INGREDIENTS •

| | |
|---|---|
| 1 small onion | 1 lb/500 g minced beef |
| 2 cloves garlic | 1 egg, size 1 or 2 |
| Small bunch parsley (enough for 2 tablespoons when chopped) | 1 oz/25 g (2 tablespoons) grated Parmesan cheese |
| Salt and pepper | A little oil |

## • METHOD •

1 Peel and finely chop the onion and garlic; wash the parsley, shake or dry with kitchen roll, and chop very finely.

2 Mix the onion, garlic, parsley, a little salt, and rather more pepper with the beef (use a fork).

3 Beat the egg smooth in a separate bowl and add to the beef. Stir in the cheese.

4 Mould the meat into flat cakes about ½ inch/1.5 cm thick and either paint with oil or roll each side in oil spread over a plate. Set the grill to medium/high; grease the bars of the pan and line the bottom with cooking foil. Grill the burgers for 4 minutes on each side or until browned all through (test with a skewer or the tip of a knife).

# • KAITY KARAGEORGIS'S • MOUSSAKA

Like Ratatouille (see page 61), this benefits from being made some hours or a day in advance so that the flavours have time to blend and develop.

In Greece, one of the cheeses used for flavouring is Kephalo-tiri, which is hard and salty. A satisfactory but rather more expensive substitute is Gruyère: failing this, try using Caerphilly (rather than Cheddar).

The proportions given here for the béchamel sauce are not the same as for Lasagne (see page 33) because a slightly stiffer sauce is needed here.

Grilling rather than frying the aubergines is suggested to save oil. If possible, allow an hour for them to sweat with salt on them before grilling. *For 4-6.*

## ▪ INGREDIENTS ▪

| | |
|---|---|
| 2 medium-sized aubergines, weighing about 1½ lb/750 g | 2 oz/50 g Parmesan cheese |
| | 3-4 tablespoons oil, preferably olive |
| Salt, some of which should be finely ground | 1 lb/500 g lean minced beef |
| 1 lb/500 g ripe tomatoes | Pepper |
| 1 large onion | Small handful parsley (enough for 1 tablespoon when chopped) |
| 2 cloves garlic | |
| 2 oz/50 g Gruyère or Caerphilly cheese | |

### BECHAMEL SAUCE

| | |
|---|---|
| 1 pint/600 ml milk | 2 oz/50 g plain white flour |
| 2 oz/50 g butter or 1 oz/25 g butter plus 2 tablespoons oil | 2 oz/50 g Gruyère or Caerphilly cheese |
| **Large baking tray** | **Largish ovenware dish** |

## ▪ METHOD ▪

**1** Wash the aubergines and cut into ⅓ inch/1 cm slices. Sprinkle a little fine salt over each slice and leave in a colander for 1 hour to sweat. Rinse under the cold tap, shake to remove surplus moisture, and allow to drain while the rest of the ingredients are being prepared.

**2** Skin and chop the tomatoes; peel and finely chop the onion and garlic; wash the parsley and shake or dry with kitchen roll, then chop. Grate all the Gruyère cheese (for both the meat and béchamel) and the Parmesan cheese, if necessary. Keep the cheeses separate.

**3** Fry the onion in 1 tablespoon oil over low heat for 10 minutes or until soft. Add the garlic and fry for another 5 minutes or until the onion begins to change colour. Put in the meat, season lightly with salt and pepper, and turn until the meat is uniformly brown and no uncooked lumps remain. Add the tomatoes with a little more seasoning and simmer for 15 minutes, stirring frequently. Remove from the heat and stir in the parsley and 2 oz/50 g of the Gruyère.

**4** Grill the aubergines. Line a plate with kitchen roll and the baking tray with cooking foil. Spread the foil with 1-1½ tablespoons oil (if the tray has no sides, turn up the edges of the foil). Blot each slice on the kitchen roll to remove any moisture and set as many as will fit without overlapping on the tray (a 12 inch/30 cm square tray will take half). Turn the slices over so that both sides are coated with a thin film of oil, set the grill to medium, and grill for 5-7 minutes per side until light brown (the slices tend to colour unevenly). Transfer the first batch to a plate, spread the foil with another 1-1½ tablespoons oil, and repeat.

**5** Arrange a third or a quarter of the aubergine over the bottom of the dish, depending on its width. Add half or a third of the Parmesan and meat sauce. Repeat the layers once or twice and top with the remaining aubergine. If to be served immediately, set the oven to 200°C, 400°F, Gas Mark 6.

**6** To make the béchamel sauce, heat, but do not boil, the milk. Put the butter or butter plus 2 tablespoons oil in a saucepan or largish frying pan and melt over gentle heat. Add the flour and stir until smooth (be careful not to allow it to brown). Pour in the milk, stirring continuously, and continue to stir until thick. Season lightly with salt and more generously with pepper, simmer about 3 minutes, then remove from the heat. Sprinkle in the 2 oz/50 g Gruyère cheese, then pour the sauce over the aubergine. (If making in advance, leave to cool, cover, and refrigerate.)

**7** Heat for 25-30 minutes or until the top begins to brown.

# · LAMB KEBABS WITH · FENNEL ·

When I first suggested giving a recipe for kebabs, the response was unfavourable because of the idea that lengthy, elaborate marinading was needed: marinading, however, is an elaboration not a necessity (though it presumably originated in the need to tenderize or disguise tough or rancid meat). The kebabs are more succulent if the ingredients are allowed 15-20 minutes to absorb oil but can perfectly well be cooked straight away.

Long skewers are necessary, plus good quality meat — but relatively little of it. A small half leg, which is a cheaper way of buying than ready-cut steaks, will provide enough not only for kebabs but Lamb with Aubergine (see page 77) and, if the bone is saved, provides the basis for soup (page 24). It can be bought boned, but this will be more expensive and cuts out the possibility of soup.

Fennel has a potent, aniseed-like taste. If this is not liked, kidneys can be used instead. As these do not stay fresh as long as ordinary meat, care should be taken to check that they are fresh; if possible, buy and cook them on the same day, but otherwise purchase them in their fat (which helps to preserve them) or check that they are firm and glossy.

Serve the kebabs with rice (see page 46). *For 4.*

## ▪ INGREDIENTS ▪

| | |
|---|---|
| 1-1¼ lb/500-625 g lamb from a small half leg or 2 large leg steaks | Salt and pepper |
| | 4 long skewers |
| 1 red pepper | Sharp, preferably smallish knife for boning a leg and/or cutting up the meat |
| 3 large or 4 small cloves garlic | |
| 4 medium ripe tomatoes | |
| 4 small or 2 large bulbs fennel, weighing 10 oz/310 g or over, or 4 lambs' kidneys | Wide, shallow ovenware dish or baking dish with slightly raised sides such as a Swiss roll tin |
| 3 tablespoons oil | |

## ▪ METHOD ▪

1 Wash the lamb in cold water; bone a half leg. With the upper half, cut the meat from round the bone in one piece; with the lower end, slice 2 or 3 steaks from the side with most of the meat, and cut down the bone to separate the remaining chunk. A little

will remain at the top: this can either be trimmed off or left for soup. Cover and put meat not needed for kebabs into the refrigrator; use the bone for stock (see page 24).

**2** If not already divided into steaks, cut the meat into slices ½ inch/1-1.5 cm thick. Trim off all visible fat and chop into 1-1¼ inch/2.5-3 cm squares.

**3** Wash and quarter the pepper; discard the white inner flesh and any seeds or dark spots and cut the flesh into even-sized squares. Peel and chop the garlic; wash the tomatoes. Chop the top and root end from the fennel, peel off the outer layer if brownish or fibrous, slice fairly thinly, and wash. If using kidneys, pull from their fat, make a shallow incision in each and peel off the inner skin; pull sharply where it is attached to the central core. Sniff to test freshness, wash, and slice thickly, cutting out or round the core. Put all the prepared ingredients except the tomatoes into a shallow bowl, cover with the oil, and leave for 15-20 minutes, basting every now and again.

**4** The kebabs can be either grilled or baked: if to be baked, set the oven to 230°C, 450°f, Gas Mark 8. Line the baking dish with cooking foil. Thread the skewers with alternate slices of ingredients (excluding garlic) with the tomato in the middle. As the layers of the fennel are not complete circles, the outer ones may fall, in which case roughly chop and return them to the bowl.

**5** Spoon the oil remaining in the bowl over the kebabs (but not the garlic or pieces of fennel) and season lightly with salt and more moderately with pepper. Bake for 10 minutes, then turn the kebabs, add the garlic and chopped fennel (which would burn if added at the beginning), baste, and bake for a further 8-10 minutes. If grilling, cook for 8-10 minutes, turning and basting every 2-3 minutes; add the garlic and fennel half-way through.

# · LAMB WITH AUBERGINE ·

This is almost Ratatouille (see page 61) with the addition of lamb: it is not a classic dish in the same way as the latter, but deserves to be.

A small half leg is better value than ready-cut steaks; the rest of the meat can be used for kebabs and the bone for soup.

Allow an hour before starting cooking for the aubergines to sweat (cooking time is 2 hours). Serve with hot bread, baked potatoes, or rice. *For 4-6.*

## ▪ INGREDIENTS ▪

| | |
|---|---|
| *2 large aubergines, weighing about 1½ lb/750 g* | *2 yellow or green peppers* |
| *Salt, some of which should be finely ground* | *1 teaspoon coriander seeds* |
| | *1 tablespoon oil, preferably olive* |
| *1-1¼ lb/500-625 g lamb from a small half leg or 2 large leg steaks* | *Pepper* |
| *1 medium onion* | *¼ pint/150 ml water plus 1 tablespoon tomato paste* |
| *3 cloves garlic* | **Casserole or ovenware dish with lid** |
| *1 lb/500 g ripe tomatoes* | |

## ▪ METHOD ▪

**1** Wash and slice the aubergines, sprinkle with fine salt, and leave to drain in a colander.

**2** Wash the lamb in cold water; bone a half leg. With the upper half, cut the meat from round the bone in one piece; with the lower, slice 2 or 3 steaks from the side with most of the meat and cut down the bone to remove the chunk at the end. A little will remain at the top; either trim off or leave for soup. Cover and refrigerate meat not immediately needed; make stock with the bone (see page 24).

**3** Trim the fat from the meat and cut into chunks about the size and thickness of chops. Peel and chop the onion, garlic, and tomatoes, discarding the tomato cores. Wash and quarter the peppers, discard the white inner flesh, pick off any seeds, and slice the flesh. Crush coriander seeds.

**4** Set the oven to 150°C, 300°F, Gas Mark 2. Rinse the aubergines under the cold tap. Cover the bottom of the casserole with the oil and put in half the aubergines, peppers, onion and garlic. Season very lightly with salt and a little more generously with pepper. Add the meat, season lightly again, then arrange the other half of the vegetables over the top. Finish with a layer of tomatoes;

season slightly a third time and sprinkle with the coriander. Mix the tomato paste with the water and pour into the casserole. Cover and bake for 2 hours; after about 1½ hours, gently turn the top layer of vegetables and press to ensure that all are submerged in the liquid.

# CHICKEN MARYLAND WITH SWEETCORN, · BACON AND BANANA ·

The difference between Chicken Maryland and Kentucky fried chicken is that, although both are coated with breadcrumbs, the Maryland version is (or can be) baked — which gives an even crisper result and, since only enough oil is needed to line the bottom of the pan, means that it is much lower in fat. Similarly, the bacon and the small amount of butter cooked with the corn hardly count compared to chips with Kentucky chicken.

The fat content of the dish is reduced still further by skinning the chicken, as most of the fat is just below the skin. If you use free-range chicken, one of the advantages is that it tends to be appreciably less fatty than battery produce.

As free-range chickens are not usually sold in portions and in any case are more economical whole (partly because the carcass provides a second meal), the first stage of the recipe is cutting up the chicken.

For the breadcrumbs stale, dry bread really is necessary — fresh bread tends to stick in lumps; if bought (uneconomical) the crumbs should be fresh, not fried.

For 4-6, depending on the size of the chicken. With a 4½-5 lb/2.25-2.5 kg one, use the larger quantities given.

## · INGREDIENTS ·

| | |
|---|---|
| 3½-5 lb/1.75-2.5 kg chicken | 4 or 6 heads corn-on-the-cob |
| A little butter | Salt and pepper |

| | |
|---|---|
| *4 oz/125 g stale bread* | *4 or 6 rashers streaky bacon* |
| *About 1 tablespoon/25 g oil* | **Shallow baking dish or tray** |
| *1 large egg* | **Skewer** |
| *About 1 oz/25 g white flour* | **Sharp, small knife** |
| *2 or 3 large bananas* | |

## ▪ METHOD ▪

**1** Remove the giblets from the chicken (usually sold in a bag inside the bird); keep the liver. Wipe the chicken inside and out with slightly dampened kitchen roll. Place it on a chopping surface (in the sink if necessary) breast, i.e. feet, downwards, and cut round the legs, preferably with a small knife, keeping as close to the ribs as possible. The joint at the top can be felt and seen; it does not need cutting and will separate with a sharp twist.
**2** Turn the bird over and cut off the breasts as near to the central (breast-) bone as possible, ending at the wings, which should not be detached but left on the carcass. If it seems easier, pull the skin (which is tougher than the flesh) from the breasts before cutting; otherwise, skin the pieces afterwards, trimming the legs at the bottom with the knife or scissors. With a larger chicken, divide the legs into thighs and drumsticks at the knee joint, which again will separate with a twist. Use the carcass and liver for Minestrone, Chicken Risotto, or Chicken Pilaff (see pages 26, 47, and 49).
**3** Set the oven to 200°C, 400°F, Gas Mark 6. Cut the crusts from the bread and grate finely; throw away any oversized scraps, which will bake unevenly.
**4** Pull the husks and hairs from the corn-on-the-cob, trim the stalks, and wash. Lightly oil or butter pieces of cooking foil large enough to wrap each head. Place on pieces of foil with a little butter and pepper (add salt after cooking as it toughens the skins if added before). Enclose in a parcel, butter uppermost.
**5** Wash and break the egg on to a large plate; season very slightly with salt and pepper and beat smooth with a fork. Spread the flour, with just a trace of seasoning, on a second large plate, and the breadcrumbs on to a third. Lightly season the chicken portions and coat, first with flour then egg, and finally crumbs;

shake off any surplus at each stage but ensure that every piece is covered all over.

**6** Peel and halve the bananas crosswise. Trim rind from the bacon, wrap a rasher round each half, at a slight angle if necessary to cover it, and secure the bacon rolls by threading on to the skewer.

**7** Line the baking dish with foil and spread with about a tablespoon of oil; arrange the chicken pieces on it with the skewer of bacon at one end (it is preferable to keep the skewer away from the chicken because moisture from the banana could affect its crispness). Put the corn parcels near the bottom of the oven and the chicken above them. Bake for 20 minutes. Turn the chicken pieces over and bake for a further 15-20 minutes. The chicken and bacon should be fairly well browned and the corn tender but still crisp.

# · CHICKEN WITH GINGER ·

Including cutting up the chicken, this takes only 15-20 minutes to prepare (5 minutes less with ready-cut portions). Serve with brown rice (see page 46), which cooks in about the same time: set it to boil as soon as the chicken is in the oven and leave it to keep hot in the saucepan if necessary.

Use grated fresh root ginger, as this gives a spicier, subtler flavour than ready ground ginger and adds a nutty texture to the sauce.

The sauce can be made with cream, yoghurt, or a mixture; cream gives a better flavour, and has the advantage of browning, which yoghurt alone will not do. A mixture of half and half gives a cream-like texture and almost as rich-tasting a result. The most desirable yoghurt for cooking is strained Greek or Greek-style, which is easily distinguished by its mild flavour and smooth texture.

To reduce the calorie content of the dish, use low-fat yoghurt (rather than Greek, which is whole-milk) and skin the chicken portions (but note that, although the appearance of the breasts is not much affected, the legs look bony and unattractive until covered with sauce).

For 4 or 6, depending on the size of the chicken. With 4½-5 lb/ 2.25-2.5 kg birds, use the larger quantities specified.

## • INGREDIENTS •

| | |
|---|---|
| 3½-5 lb/1.75-2.5 kg chicken | 2 or 3 cloves garlic |
| 1 or 2 green or yellow peppers | ¼ or ⅜ pint/150 or 230 ml double cream, yoghurt stabilized with 1 teaspoon flour, or a mixture, plus 2 or 3 tablespoons milk |
| 4 or 6 courgettes | |
| 1½-2 inch/4-5 cm piece fresh root ginger | |
| | **Shallow ovenware dish** |
| 1 or 1½ teaspoons coriander seeds or ½ teaspoon ground | **Sharp, short knife for cutting up the chicken** |
| 2 or 3 tablespoons oil | |
| Salt and pepper | |

## • METHOD •

**1** Set the oven to 200°C, 400°F, Gas Mark 6. Cut up the chicken in the same way as for Chicken Maryland with Sweetcorn, Bacon and Banana (see page 79).

**2** Wash the pepper and courgettes. Slice the courgettes; quarter, core, and remove inner flesh and any seeds from the pepper and slice finely. Peel the ginger; crush the coriander seeds in a pestle and mortar.

**3** Cover the bottom of the dish with oil, arrange the slices of courgettes and pepper in it in an even layer, then sprinkle with the coriander. Add the chicken pieces. Coarsely grate in the peeled ginger, season with salt and pepper to taste, and bake for 30 minutes.

**4** Peel and chop the garlic. Take the dish from the oven, shutting the door so that heat is not lost, remove the chicken, and turn the courgettes, which should be golden on the underside. Sprinkle the garlic over the bottom of the dish, return the chicken, and bake for 5 more minutes. Pour the cream or yoghurt over the chicken and cook for a further 5-8 minutes, until the cream is bubbling and just beginning to change its colour. Serve immediately.

# CHICKEN AND
# · CHILLI CASSEROLE ·

---

This dish is as low-fat as is possible with chicken: the pieces are skinned — not only to save calories but because the skin becomes tough and stringy in stews — none of the ingredients is pre-fried (which also saves time), nor is any oil added.

The flavour is subtle rather than strong: the chilli and paprika are perceptible but do not mask the taste of the chicken.

The casserole can be made in advance and reheated. Serve with hot bread, pasta (see page 29), rice (see page 46), or potatoes. Baked potatoes can be cooked at the same time: put medium to largish ones, i.e. 8-10 oz/250-310 g, into the oven 15-20 minutes after the casserole on the shelf above. Use a floury variety, e.g. King Edward, Cara or Pentland Squire as these are particularly good for mopping up the casserole liquid.

For 4-6, depending on the size of chicken. The quantities of other ingredients need no alteration.

## · INGREDIENTS ·

| | |
|---|---|
| 3½-5 lb/1.75-2.5 kg chicken | ¼ pint/150 ml water |
| 8oz/250 g ripe tomatoes | Salt |
| 1 medium onion | 1 level teaspoon paprika |
| 2-3 cloves garlic | 1 teaspoon dried thyme or mixed herbs |
| 1 red and 1 green pepper | |
| 1 green chilli | **Medium-large casserole** |
| 4 oz/125 g mushrooms | **Sharp, short knife for dividing the chicken** |
| 1 tablespoon tomato paste | |

## · METHOD ·

**1** Cut up the chicken in the same way as for Chicken Maryland with Sweetcorn, Bacon and Banana (see page 79).

**2** Peel and chop the tomatoes, onion, and garlic. Wash and quarter the peppers and chilli; discard the seeds and white inner flesh and cut into strips. Trim the stalks of the mushrooms, wash small, or peel and wipe large ones, and slice coarsely or leave whole according to size. Mix together all the vegetables except the tomatoes.

**3** Set the oven to 200°C, 400°F, Gas Mark 6. Dissolve the tomato paste in the water. Put the chicken pieces in the bottom of the casserole, season with salt and paprika, and sprinkle with the herbs. Place the mixed vegetables over them in a thick layer; add the tomatoes and pour the dissolved paste over the top. Cover and bake for 1 hour 25 minutes. When ready, a plentiful quantity of rich-looking sauce will have formed and the chicken should come easily from the bone. If serving later, reheat at the same temperature for 25-30 minutes, until the sauce bubbles all over. (Making sure that the temperature is high enough is very important as boiling ensures that bacteria cannot survive.)

# · ROAST CHICKEN WITH · BASIL BUTTER

As the chicken is not cut up but plainly roasted, very little preparation is involved: if you grow your own basil, the dish also costs almost nothing beyond the bird itself — but will need an accompaniment of potatoes (new or baked with the chicken) and a vegetable, which can be virtually anything (peas, cauliflower, broccoli, spinach, or a green salad).

Pick the leaves lower down rather than at the top of the basil stems as you will do less damage to the plant.

*For* 4-6, depending on the size of the chicken: with a chicken of 4½-5 lb/2.25-2.5 kg, use the larger quantities given.

## · INGREDIENTS ·

| | |
|---|---|
| *8-12 basil leaves* | *3½-5 lb/1.75-2.5 kg chicken* |
| *2-3 small cloves garlic* | *Salt and pepper* |

| 2-3 oz/50-90 g butter, preferably unsalted | **Roasting pan or shallow ovenware dish** |

### • METHOD •

**1** Set the oven to 200°C, 400°F, Gas Mark 6. Wash the basil and leave to drain on kitchen roll. Peel and roughly chop 1 of the cloves of garlic.

**2** Line the pan or dish with cooking foil. Remove the giblets from the chicken, keeping the liver, and wipe the bird inside and out with moistened kitchen roll. Set breast upwards in the pan. Roughly chop 1 clove of garlic and tear 2 or 3 basil leaves into pieces: put into the cavity of the bird to flavour it as it cooks. Sprinkle lightly with salt and pepper and roast. Roasting times are 20 minutes per lb plus 15 minutes for a bird weighing 3½-4 lb/1.75-2 kg; 20 minutes per lb plus 10 minutes for 4½-5 lb/2.25-2.5 kg (i.e. a 3½ lb/1.75 kg chicken needs 1 hour 25 minutes, a 4 lb/2 kg one 1 hour 35 minutes, a 4½ lb/2.25 kg one 1 hour 40 minutes, or a 5 lb/2.5 kg one 1 hour 50 minutes). These times are generous but it is important that the chicken is thoroughly cooked to kill any bacteria which may be present. Check the bird 3 or 4 times during roasting and turn to ensure even cooking. When ready, it should be crisp and well browned and the juices coagulated throughout the bird; test by inserting a fine skewer or the point of a knife into the breast as far as the ribs: any liquid that comes out should run clear without any trace of pink.

**3** Tear the rest of the basil leaves into pieces and roughly chop the remaining 1-2 cloves of garlic. Put into a pestle and mortar with the butter, season moderately generously with salt and pepper (or with salt to taste if the butter is already salted) and crush: if the butter is straight from the refrigerator, dice before crushing.

**4** To carve the chicken, cut off the legs, separating the joint at the bottom with a sharp twist; divide the legs at the knee; slice the breast diagonally from the centre bone. Serve with a knob of basil butter on each portion.

**5** Boil the carcass and chicken liver for stock (see page 28); if much meat is left over, use it in the recipe for Chicken in Béchamel (see page 86).

# · CHICKEN IN BÉCHAMEL ·

The point of this recipe is that for the price of the mushrooms (not counting basic ingredients) it turns left-over pieces of chicken into an excellent meal. Roast or boiled chicken from a carcass can be used; stock is not needed.

Altogether, it takes 30 minutes for 2 or (because of preparing more vegetables) about 35 minutes for 4. Serve with rice (see page 46) or new potatoes. As brown rice needs to cook for 30-35 minutes, put it on just before starting. Scrub potatoes before chopping the onion and set them to boil while frying the onion.

If your quantity of left-over chicken is less than 2 oz/50 g per person it is not worth making this dish; instead, add the chicken to the stuffing for Mushroom Pancakes (see page 66).

If possible, choose large mushrooms, which tend to have more flavour than button ones. *For 2.*

## · INGREDIENTS ·

| | |
|---|---|
| 1 small onion | ½ oz/15 g butter or 1 tablespoon oil |
| 1-2 cloves garlic | Salt and pepper |
| 4 oz/125 g mushrooms, preferably large | Scant ½ oz/12 g flour (white thickens more smoothly but brown tastes more interesting) |
| 4 oz/125 g cooked chicken | |
| ½ pint/300 ml milk | 1 teaspoon mild French mustard (e.g. Grey Poupon) |
| Bay leaf (optional) | |

## · METHOD ·

**1** Peel and finely chop the onion and garlic. Wipe mushrooms, peel if large, then slice. Chop the chicken into smallish, even-sized pieces, discarding any gristle or skin — particularly if using chicken left over from Chicken with Orange and Brandy (see page 156), which will be slightly sweet.

**2** Heat the milk, with the bay leaf if using; do not allow to boil (heating extracts the flavour of the leaf but is helpful even without one because if the milk is warmed before use the sauce will thicken more quickly).

**3** Fry the onion slowly in the butter or oil, turning often, for 10 minutes or until soft. Add the garlic and mushrooms, season lightly with salt and pepper and continue frying for 5-7 minutes or until the mushrooms are soft. Stir in the flour and, as soon as it is smooth (it is important that it should not brown), slowly pour in the milk, stirring continuously. Continue to stir until the sauce thickens (if it takes longer than 3-5 minutes, raise the heat a little). Add the mustard and chicken, season lightly again, and simmer for another 2 or 3 minutes. Serve at once.

# · QUICK PORK CASSEROLE ·

This makes a change from the eternal grilled pork chop and, although it needs long cooking, is quick to prepare because all you have to do is wash and chop the vegetables. Serve with new potatoes. *For 4.*

## · INGREDIENTS ·

| | |
|---|---|
| *4 pork chops* | *2 teaspoons dried mixed herbs or oregano* |
| *12 oz-1 lb/375-500 g leeks* | |
| *8 oz/250 g carrots* | *Salt and pepper* |
| *2 small turnips or 4 sticks celery* | *2 tablespoons tomato paste* |
| *4 oz/125 g mushrooms (large or small)* | *½ pint/300 ml water* |
| | **Largish casserole or ovenware dish with lid** |
| *2-3 cloves garlic* | |

## · METHOD ·

**1** Wash the chops and trim off the outside fat.

**2** Chop the root and leaves from the leeks, slice into ½ inch/ 1.5 cm slices, and wash; peel and roughly slice the carrots. Trim the root ends and leaves from the celery, wash, and slice; peel and chop turnips into ½ inch/1.5 cm squares. Wash small, or

peel and wipe large, mushrooms, and slice thickly; peel and finely chop the garlic. Set the oven to 150°C, 300°F, Gas Mark 2.
**3** Mix the prepared vegetables and put half into the casserole; add the chops, sprinkle with 1 teaspoon of the mixed herbs or oregano, a generous seasoning of pepper, and rather less salt. Add the rest of the vegetables, season lightly again, and sprinkle with the rest of the herbs.
**4** Dissolve the tomato paste in the water and pour into the casserole. Bake 1½ hours. Turn the vegetables and continue to bake for another 35-45 minutes, until the chops are coming off the bone and the sauce is rich and dark.

# · MACKEREL WITH · ALMONDS

Compared to most other fish, mackerel are wonderfully cheap, and also healthy, since they contain oil, unlike white fish such as cod. Fish oil is supposedly the reason why Eskimos do not suffer from heart disease.

Fresh mackerel have a rich rather than fishy taste — but they must be absolutely fresh. When fresh, they look shiny and glossy, and are hard and firm, with no smell at all. They should be eaten on the day of purchase, or at any rate not kept for more than 12 hours: put them at the bottom of the refrigerator on a plate covered with greaseproof paper or another plate. Normally, the fishmonger will offer to clean, i.e. gut, them: otherwise, do this directly after buying. Do not store them uncleaned.

There are lots of ways of cooking them, but the best and easiest is grilling which takes less than 15 minutes. *Per person.*

## · INGREDIENTS ·

| | |
|---|---|
| *10-12 oz/310-375 g mackerel* | *Salt and pepper* |
| *½ oz/12 g (¼ of a 50 g packet) flaked almonds* | **Sharp knife if the fish are not cleaned** |
| *A very little butter* | |

# • METHOD •

**1** Clean the fish if necessary. Cut off the head behind the gills and slit the underneath from the head end to about two-thirds of the way to the tail. Lift out the gut on the flat of the knife, scraping to remove the dark matter at the back: rinse in cold water, check that the fish is clean, and if any dark spots remain, scrape and rinse again.

**2** Remove the grid from the grill pan and line the pan with cooking foil. Set the grill to medium. Scatter the almonds over the bottom of the pan and toast for about 20 seconds, when (unless the grill is not yet fully heated) they will already be beginning to change colour; remove, shake, and toast for another 10-20 seconds, until slightly browned (toasting them dry in advance gives a crisper result than tossing them over the fish with its oil at the end). Empty them from the pan but keep the pan covered with foil; do not turn off the grill.

**3** Wash the fish in cold water inside and out and wipe dry with kitchen roll (if just washed after cleaning, there is no need to wash the inside again). Make 4 or 5 cuts about ½ inch/1.5 cm deep at intervals across each side (this is to ensure even cooking). Rub all over with just enough butter to grease them, using a piece of buttered kitchen roll. Season each side with a little salt and pepper and lay in the grill pan. (I suggest not using the grid of the pan because the smell may cling to the uncovered bars, but you can use it if you like, in which case rub the bars with butter and wipe with the cut side of half a lemon afterwards. However, bear in mind that the closer the fish is to the heat, the more likely the skin will be to char.)

**4** Grill each side for 5-7 minutes. The side is done when the flesh flakes easily to the bone when tested with the point of a knife; the skin should be crisp and brown. Shake the almonds over the fish and put back under the grill to heat for a few seconds: watch carefully. Serve immediately. If in spite of the foil the pan smells of mackerel, rub with lemon before washing.

# · KIPPERS WITH CRISP · POTATO

The kippers involve virtually no preparation at all: simply wipe them and put them in the oven. For a really easy meal, serve with plain baked rather than the baked mashed potatoes given here: the latter can be prepared in advance, nor need they be baked so long, but a really crisp finish takes at least 40 minutes.

Try to buy undyed kippers and use floury potatoes such as King Edward, Cara or Pentland Squire.

Butter is recommended for this recipe as it gives a better flavour, but you can use margarine. *For 4.*

## · INGREDIENTS ·

| | |
|---|---|
| 2 lb/500 g potatoes | 4 kippers |
| Salt and pepper | **Large shallow ovenware dish or a baking tray** |
| ¼ pint/150 ml milk | |
| 2-3 oz/50-90 g butter | **Medium-sized deeper ovenware dish** |
| 4 moderately-ripe tomatoes (optional) | |

## · METHOD ·

**1** Peel and quarter the potatoes and boil in slightly salted water for 20 minutes or until soft. Set the oven to 200°C, 400°F, Gas Mark 6. Grease the deeper ovenware dish.

**2** Drain and mash the potatoes. Stir in the milk, ½ oz/15 g of the butter, and season with salt and pepper. Turn into the prepared dish, rough the top with a fork, and dot with another ½-1 oz/15-25 g butter. Bake for 40-45 minutes, until well browned.

**3** Wash the tomatoes, slice off the tops, and cut out the cores. Grease the shallow dish or line a baking tray with greased foil turned up at the edges to form a raised rim. Wipe the kippers with damp kitchen roll and arrange on the dish with the tomatoes. Rub or dot the kippers with a little butter and place a tablespoon of milk in the middle of each one. Season the tomatoes slightly with salt and more generously with pepper and moisten with a little butter.

**4** When the potatoes have been baking for 35 minutes, or are already fairly brown, put the kippers into the oven. Bake for 8-10 minutes until the kippers flake easily with a fork but are still firm. Serve immediately with the potatoes and tomatoes.

# · SALADS ·

Salads can be made not only from conventional ingredients but almost anything: the only vegetables which spring to mind as unsuitable (cooked or uncooked) are parsnips and swedes. Many of the recipes do not include lettuce, partly because, although an increasingly large number of varieties are available, all are relatively expensive except the conventional round sort and, while often decorative (notably the red types), tend to have very little flavour. Probably the best value are the large, crisp, sweet Cos; of the same type but very small and relatively dear are Little Gem, which are almost all heart. I have included tomatoes mainly for texture and slight tartness. In the interests of the latter, choose those which are firm and less ripe rather than the softer ones recommended for sauce.

Age or ripeness is important with many items: avocado pears (like ordinary pears) are at the right stage for only about a day; baby turnips are delicious raw but older ones fibrous, and new carrots a seasonal treat (and if untrimmed, with still firm and glossy leaves, probably fresh — but dearer). Button mushrooms have less flavour than larger, open ones, but are better for salads because of their firmer texture.

As the quality of the vegetables is all important, recipes are intended merely as guides or suggestions rather than hard-and-fast formulae. If the radicchio on sale looks brown and flaccid (or is too expensive), use something else with a bitter flavour, such as chicory, or a few leaves of spinach, or omit it altogether. Weary lettuces, herbs and carrots will often revive in cold water, but not wrinkled peppers or spinach so tired that the leaves have collapsed. Stale cucumbers are difficult to detect until eaten, when the skin will be tough — in which case, peel them. Avoid lettuces with crinkly brown edges to the leaves; the brown may not be only on the outside but go all the way through.

On the question of health, I can only point out that pesticide residues are not reported to be removed by cooking — whereas vitamins definitely are. The bad news is that (along with apples) lettuces, tomatoes, and potatoes have been found to retain particularly high levels. All that can be done is to wash as much as possible from the surface, soak vegetables to be cooked (such as French beans) in hot water, and buy organically grown or unsprayed produce if possible. (Organic produce, because it is untreated, will not keep as long.)

When preparing salads, wash items in advance and leave them to drain in a sieve or colander but, unless to be flavoured and/or softened by marinating in dressing, leave slicing or chopping until just before the meal or they will lose not only their freshness but also some of their vitamins. Similarly, dressing can be made whenever convenient but should not be added until the last moment. The classic dressing, which is suitable for most salads, is French dressing; with this, there really is no substitute for olive oil. For thicker dressings, yoghurt and cheese can be added (the classic thick dressing, mayonnaise, is both very expensive and fattening because of the amount of oil needed; it is also made with raw egg, so must be made with very fresh eggs from a reliable source to avoid the risk of salmonella. Suggested lower-calorie dressings are Yoghurt or Lemon and Tomato (see below). Alternatively, salads can be sprinkled with plain lemon juice or not dressed at all, which is fine for some salads but would make others inedibly dreary.

# · FRENCH DRESSING ·

## · INGREDIENTS ·

4 tablespoons olive oil

Salt and pepper

1 tablespoon red or white wine vinegar

## · METHOD ·

Mix all the ingredients together, adding a moderate amount of seasoning. Since the oil and vinegar do not blend, beat again with a fork just before serving.

# · YOGHURT DRESSING ·

## · INGREDIENTS ·

2 tablespoons olive oil

¾ tablespoon wine vinegar

Salt and pepper

A very little caster or soft brown sugar (optional)

¼ pint/150 ml or 4 oz/125 g (small carton) natural yoghurt, preferably mild (Greek or Greek-style is especially recommended but low-fat can be used)

## · METHOD ·

Mix together the oil and vinegar, then add to the yoghurt (rather than the other way round: thick-set yoghurt, if added to the liquid, will refuse to blend and have to be sieved). Beat until smooth, then season with a little salt and more pepper; taste, and if sharp add up to ¼ teaspoon sugar (the amount needed will depend on the flavour of the yoghurt).

# · LEMON AND TOMATO DRESSING ·

## · INGREDIENTS ·

| | |
|---|---|
| *8 oz/250 g ripe tomatoes* | *1 tablespoon olive oil* |
| *1 small or ½ large lemon* | *Salt and black pepper* |

## · METHOD ·

Skin, finely chop, and sieve the tomatoes. With energetic pressing, almost all the flesh will liquidize. Stir in the lemon juice, oil, and a little seasoning with a fork. (This has the bonus of a particularly attractive rosy colour.)

# · LEMON DRESSING ·

## · INGREDIENTS ·

| | |
|---|---|
| *Juice of 1 large lemon* | *Salt and black pepper (preferably freshly ground)* |
| *¼ pint/150 ml olive oil* | |

## · METHOD ·

Mix the ingredients as for French Dressing (see page 94).

# · GARLIC DRESSING ·

## · INGREDIENTS ·

| | |
|---|---|
| *1 small clove garlic* | *French Dressing (see page 94)* |

## · METHOD ·

Peel, chop and pound the garlic in a pestle and mortar. Add the French Dressing to the mortar (this is easier than transferring the garlic to the dressing). Stir thoroughly.

# · SYDNA'S BEAN AND · SPINACH SALAD

This is a substantial and nutritious salad served with crusty bread but very refreshing because of the lemon. The inclusion of mushrooms, which are very absorbent, means that a generous quantity of dressing is needed: low-fat Lemon and Tomato Dressing (see page 95), however, can be substituted for the lemon dressing given.

White kidney beans can be cooked without soaking, in which case 2 hours' simmering is required; otherwise, soak the beans overnight.

Two hours should also be allowed for the salad (or part of it) to marinate before serving.

White-stemmed sea-kale beet can be used instead of spinach but is less tender. *For 4.*

## · INGREDIENTS ·

| | |
|---|---|
| 8 oz/250 g white kidney or haricot beans | 8 oz/250 g button mushrooms |
| | 1 green or yellow pepper |
| Salt | 4 firm tomatoes |
| 4 oz/125 g spinach (if only 1 lb/ 500 g packs are available, pick over and wash the whole quantity and store the surplus in the refrigerator, where it will stay fresh for several days) | A few cherry tomatoes (optional) |
| | Lemon or Lemon and Tomato Dressing (see page 95) |

## · METHOD ·

**1** Rinse the beans (soaked or not) under the tap. Cover with unsalted water, bring to the boil, and skim. Boil kidney beans for 10 minutes, then reduce the heat and simmer for 30 minutes or until tender, if soaked beans, or 1¾-2 hours if unsoaked; simmer haricot beans for 50-60 minutes. Add a little salt and simmer 5 minutes more.

**2** Meanwhile, break off the spinach stems close to the leaves (or cut them out from beet) and trim the mushroom stalks. Wash all the vegetables (muddy spinach may need an extra rinse) and leave to drain.

**3** Make the dressing.

**4** Drain the cooked beans. Unless the leaves are very small, tear the spinach into pieces and arrange in a salad bowl or individual bowls. Add the beans while still warm. Finely slice the mushrooms and place on top. Stir the dressing, pour about two-thirds over them, and leave for 2 hours, basting the mushrooms with the dressing every now and again.

**5** Shortly before serving, slice the tomatoes, cutting out the hard cores. Either quarter the pepper or cut off the stalk end, remove the core, seeds, and inner flesh, and slice into sticks or rounds. Arrange over the mushrooms. Top with cherry tomatoes (if used) and add the rest of the dressing.

# · MUSHROOM AND · PEPPER SALAD

This can be made as a side salad consisting of raw vegetables only, or as a main course with fish or broad beans. Pasta shells or macaroni can also be added.

As with Sydna's Bean and Spinach Salad (see page 96), the absorbency of the mushrooms means that a relatively large amount of dressing is needed; 1 quantity of low-fat Lemon and Tomato Dressing (see page 95) can be used, if preferred.

Allow an hour or so for the mushrooms and spinach to marinate. *For 4.*

## · INGREDIENTS ·

| | |
|---|---|
| *4 oz/125 g spinach (white-stemmed sea-kale beet can be used if necessary)* | *2 green peppers* |
| | *Small handful basil leaves or 2 or 3 stems fresh dill* |
| *12 oz/375 g button mushrooms* | |

| | |
|---|---|
| 6 oz/190 g pasta (optional) | 8-12 oz/250-375 g fresh or frozen filleted cod or haddock or 1 lb/500 g broad beans (optional) |
| Salt | |
| 1½-2 quantities Garlic Dressing (see page 95) according to whether additional ingredients are included | 4 leaves of radicchio (optional) |

## • METHOD •

1 Tear off (or with beet, cut out) the stems; trim the mushroom stalks. Wash the vegetables and herbs, and leave to drain.

2 Cook the pasta if it is to be included (see page 29). Toss the pasta in the dressing while still hot.

3 Finely slice the mushrooms and tear spinach into pieces. Add to the pasta and dressing, toss gently, then leave to marinate.

4 Cook the fish, or beans if using. With fresh fish, skin if necessary and either bake or simmer. To bake, season with salt and pepper, enclose in a parcel of foil, and cook at 200°C, 400°F, Gas Mark 6 for 20 minutes or until the flesh flakes easily with a fork; to simmer, just cover with slightly salted water, bring to the boil, and simmer for 7-12 minutes (time depends on thickness). Follow directions on the wrapper for frozen fish. Divide the cooked fish into small chunks and add to the salad. If using beans, pod, then cook in boiling salted water for 15-25 minutes. Skin large ones, if preferred. Add to the salad.

5 Shortly before serving, cut off the stalk end of the peppers, remove core, seeds, and white inner flesh, and slice into rounds. Tear radicchio into pieces; remove stem and chop dill or tear basil leaves. Toss lightly into the salad, reserving a few rounds of pepper and a sprinkling of herbs for the top.

# CELERY AND
# • GORGONZOLA SALAD •

This is a chunky, satisfying salad which is fairly quick to prepare (no cooking of vegetables, marinading of mushrooms, or chopping of herbs is entailed).

Stilton or another type of hard blue cheese can be used as a substitute for Gorgonzola. *For 4.*

### ▪ INGREDIENTS ▪

| | |
|---|---|
| 1 *head celery* | 6 *oz/190 g Gorgonzola cheese* |
| 2 *heads chicory* | 2 *large eating apples,* |
| 4 *leaves of radicchio or* 1 *slice red cabbage* | *preferably* Cox |
| 4 *small or* 2 *medium carrots, weighing about* 4 *oz/125 g* | *French or Yoghurt Dressing (see page 94)* |

### ▪ METHOD ▪

**1** Pull the celery stalks from the root, discarding any fibrous or brownish outer stems. Cut off the leaf end and remove further discoloured patches. Chop the root from the chicory, separate the leaves and remove any brown tips or streaks. Halve the hearts. Remove the outer layer of cabbage, if using. Scrub and peel the carrots and wash the other vegetables.
**2** Chop the celery and chicory into slices; finely slice the carrot; dice the cabbage or tear radicchio into pieces. Put into a salad bowl or individual bowls. Crumble or dice the cheese and add.
**3** Just before serving, wash, quarter and core the apples, then chop into squares (if cut sooner, they will discolour). Add to the salad. Beat the dressing with a fork, pour over the salad and toss.

# ▪ RED SALAD ▪

The red lettuce is an extravagance — but the colour combination irresistible. Except on the rare occasion when a red lettuce really has flavour, green lettuce is just as satisfactory gastronomically and colour contrast can be supplied by substituting a few dark red or green radicchio or spinach leaves. If using a large oakleaf lettuce half may be enough; use outside leaves, rinse the rest, and keep until next day in a food bag in the refrigerator. Be sure to finish it up quickly to enjoy it at its best.

If the tomatoes are well flavoured, the salad does not need dressing. For 4.

## ▪ INGREDIENTS ▪

| | |
|---|---|
| 2 heads chicory | About 4 inch/10 cm piece cucumber |
| 1 oakleaf, Italian Lollo Rosso, or other red lettuce (only the tips of Lollo Rosso leaves are red) | Bunch spring onions |
| Small handful parsley | 8 oz/250 g carrots |
| 1 lb/500 g firm tomatoes | Salt and pepper |
| 1 red pepper | |

## ▪ METHOD ▪

**1** Cut the root end from the chicory and separate the heads as far as the heart. Trim off any withered tips or edges to the leaves; halve the heart. Pull the leaves from the lettuce. Wash the parsley and all the vegetables except the onions and carrots, and leave to drain. Top and tail and peel the outer layer from the onions; scrub or peel the carrots.

**2** Slice or quarter the tomatoes, cutting out the hard cores, and put into a salad bowl and season with a little salt and pepper. Slice the onions and cucumber and add; season very slightly again with salt and pepper.

**3** Quarter the pepper, remove core, seeds, white inner flesh and any dark spots, then dice into small pieces. Dice the cheese. Cut the carrot into sticks or slice; chop the chicory leaves into short lengths (put several inside each other so that they can be chopped together). Add the prepared ingredients to the salad bowl. Tear the lettuce into pieces and chop the parsley. Add to the bowl and toss gently.

**Variation** Add all or any of the following to the salad:
    2 baby turnips, peeled and diced
    4-6 oz/125-190 g Caerphilly, Edam, low-fat or mild Cheddar, or other cheese
    French Dressing (in which case you should not include the salt and pepper).

# · PURPLE SALAD ·

The chief ingredient in this salad is red cabbage, which is as effective as red lettuce in providing the basis for a striking colour combination. *For* 4.

## · INGREDIENTS ·

| | |
|---|---|
| *12 oz–1 lb/375–500 g red cabbage* | *1 oz/25 g sunflower seeds* |
| *2 sticks celery* | *2 oz/50 g walnut halves or pieces* |
| *1 red pepper* | *1 oz/25 g raisins* |
| *2 large or 4 small carrots* | *Yoghurt Dressing (see page 94)* |
| *8 firm tomatoes, weighing about 1¼ lb/625 g* | |

## · METHOD ·

**1** Remove the outer leaves from the cabbage, trim the root end, cut off the required amount in slices (probably 2-3), and wash. Pull the celery sticks from the head; chop off the leaves, slice away any brown patches, and wash. Wash and quarter the pepper, cutting out the white inner flesh and any dark spots and discarding the seeds. Peel or scrub the carrots; wash the tomatoes. Set the oven to 200°C, 400°F, Gas Mark 6.

**2** Roughly chop the walnuts. Shred the cabbage, discarding the hard, thick stem near the bottom; slice the celery; thinly slice or chop the carrots into matchsticks (slicing is quicker); slice and then cut out the hard core of the tomatoes; dice the pepper into small squares.

**3** Put the sunflower seeds and the walnuts on baking trays and bake the sunflower seeds for 3-4 minutes and the walnuts for 4-5 minutes until crisp and just (but only just) beginning to change colour.

**4** Put all the prepared ingredients and the raisins into a salad bowl or individual bowls. Toss the dressing into a single salad just before serving or place a dollop on top of each bowl.

# · GREEN SALAD ·

Virtually by definition, this is intended as an accompaniment rather than a meal and it can, therefore, be extremely simple. In restaurants, it may be relatively elaborate, with several sorts of salad leaves. However, lettuce or another vegetable with just one or two additions to give it interest is all that is needed. My suggestions are: lettuce with chives and perhaps radishes, beans with spring onions, and leeks with olives.

## · LETTUCE WITH CHIVES ·

In this case, a recipe as such is unnecessary. For 4, simply wash a slim wand of chives and a lettuce (or ½ a large Cos) and top, tail and wash a bunch of radishes, if desired. Tear (rather than cut) the lettuce into pieces, finely chop the chives and slice or leave radishes whole. Dress and toss just before serving.

## · BEANS WITH ONIONS ·

Any sort of green bean can be used, including runner beans.
 The quantity used here is generous; depending on the rest of the meal, 12 oz/375 g may be enough. For 4.

### · INGREDIENTS ·

| | |
|---|---|
| 1 lb/500 g beans | French Dressing (see page 94) |
| Salt | 1 bunch spring onions |

### · METHOD ·
1. Top and tail non-string beans, wash, and cook in boiling salted water for 5-8 minutes or until just tender but still a little crisp. Runner beans need stringing, chopping into shortish lengths, and boiling for 20-25 minutes.

**2.** Pour the dressing over the beans while still warm.

**3.** Cut the root and leaf ends from the onions and peel off the outer layer (including the slippery inner skin). Slice fairly thinly and scatter over the beans.

## · LEEKS WITH OLIVES ·

The size of olives varies — with smallish ones, 2 oz/50 g will give 4-5 each. *For 4.*

### · INGREDIENTS ·

| | |
|---|---|
| *2 lb/1 kg leeks* | *Salt* |
| *2 or 3 oz/50 or 90 g black olives, preferably mildly salted* | *French Dressing (see page 94)* |

### · METHOD ·

**1** Cut the roots and green tops from the leeks and peel off the outer layer. Chop into 2 inch/5 cm lengths and slit to the middle but do not pull apart. Slitting makes it easier to wash the mud from between the layers, but keep the stems whole, since if they separate the salad looks floppy and unappetizing. Wash well.

**2** Cook in boiling salted water for 5-6 minutes, until only just tender; drain carefully but thoroughly.

**3** Make the dressing and pour it over the leeks while they are still warm. Put into individual bowls and stud with olives.

## JOE ALLEN'S RED ONION AND ·WATERCRESS SALAD·

Joe Allen's is an American restaurant in London notable for salads and beefburgers — and the following is absolutely the

perfect partner for the latter (see page 72). It also goes especially
well with Walnut Bread (see page 116). The restaurant was not
asked to supply the recipe — there was no need.

The balance of flavours depends on the piquancy of cherry
tomatoes against the onions. Red onions are milder than the
usual white ones, but the salad is still potent.

Watercress bought in an airtight box or bag from the supermarket can be stored in the refrigerator in the box or bag,
otherwise, pick over, trim, and wash it as for immediate use and
put into an airtight bag before refrigerating. *For* 4.

## ▪ INGREDIENTS ▪

| | |
|---|---|
| 8-12 oz/250-375 g cherry tomatoes, depending on size (they are usually sold in 8-oz/250-g packs; with really tiny ones one pack is plenty, but if they are larger it is desirable to have more, since you want at least 7 or 8 per person) | 1 large bunch watercress |
| | 4 red onions |
| | French Dressing (see page 94) |

## ▪ METHOD ▪

Pick over the watercress, trim the stalks and wash. Wash the
tomatoes and peel and slice the onions. Arrange in a salad bowl
or individual bowls. Make the dressing and add just before
serving, stirring well.

# ▪ AVOCADO AND CRISP ▪ BACON SALAD

This is an example of the now-fashionable 'warm' salads — the
croûtons and bacon being cooked just before serving so that
they are absolutely fresh and still warm.

The avocados should give slightly to the touch, when handled,
without being too soft. Do not buy any that have squashy
patches. If they are hard, keep at room temperature until they
ripen and soften. *For* 4.

## • INGREDIENTS •

| | |
|---|---|
| ½ a Cos lettuce or 2 Little Gem, or other crisp lettuce | 4 slices stale bread |
| 3 or 4 leaves of radicchio | 2 avocado pears |
| 4 firm tomatoes | French Dressing (see page 94) |
| 8 oz/250 g streaky bacon | |

## • METHOD •

**1** Wash the lettuce, radicchio, and tomatoes and leave to drain.
**2** Set the oven to 200°C, 400°F, Gas Mark 6. Using kitchen scissors, snip the rind from the bacon and cut the bacon into smallish squares. Cut the crusts from the bread and chop it into slightly smaller squares. Spread both sets of squares on a baking tray: there is no need to grease it or add fat.
**3** Tear the lettuce and radicchio leaves into pieces and arrange on the serving plates. Slice the tomatoes and cut the slices in half, removing hard centres of core. Arrange on top of the lettuce. Halve the avocados, remove the stones, and peel.
**4** Put the bread and bacon squares into the oven and bake for 7-10 minutes or until the bacon is crisp and the croûtons golden.
**5** Meanwhile, cut the avocado into slices and place on top of the tomato (this must be done shortly before serving because avocado tends to turn brown on exposure to air). Remove the bacon and croûtons from the oven and scatter a quarter on top of each salad. Beat the dressing with a fork, pour it over, and serve immediately.

# • BROAD BEAN AND • BACON SALAD

When broad beans are in season (July-August) make this salad instead of Avocado and Crisp Bacon Salad (see page 101). Partly because of the inclusion of potatoes, it is both more satisfying and also more nutritious. Its oil, and hence also calorie content, can be reduced by using Lemon and Tomato Dressing (see page 95) rather than French Dressing.

If possible, use waxier potatoes, e.g. Maris Bard, Maris Piper, Ulster Sceptre (late May-end July), Desirée or Pentland Crown (September-April), rather than the flourier varieties (King Edward, Cara, and Pentland Squire), which are sometimes crumbly even when new. Do not be tempted to cook the beans and potatoes together as the beans will make the potatoes grey.

The potatoes are dressed while still hot so that they absorb the flavour of the dressing. *For 4.*

## ▪ INGREDIENTS ▪

| | |
|---|---|
| 1 lb/500 g broad beans | A few parsley sprigs |
| Salt | 4 slices stale bread for croûtons |
| 1 lb/500 g new potatoes | 4 firm tomatoes |
| 8 oz/250 g streaky bacon | ½ a Cos lettuce or 2 Little Gem, or other crisp lettuce |
| French Dressing (see page 94) or Lemon and Tomato Dressing (see page 95) | 3 or 4 leaves of radicchio |

## ▪ METHOD ▪

**1** Pod the beans and cook in boiling salted water until tender; they will take 15-25 minutes according to age and size. If very large, rinse under the cold tap and peel (this tip comes from Jane Grigson's *Vegetable Book*; it is not essential but is, at least in gastronomic terms, a great improvement).

**2** Scrub and remove any green patches from the potatoes but do not peel. Cook in boiling salted water for 15-20 minutes until just soft. (It is healthier and more interesting to leave them unpeeled, but in any case if they are for eating cold they can be peeled, in the same way as scalded tomatoes, after cooking. Not only are their vitamins retained but they are also less crumbly.)

**3** Make the dressing. Wash the parsley and the rest of the vegetables and leave to drain.

**4** As soon as the potatoes are cool enough to handle, slice and lay in the bottom of either one large bowl or 4 separate bowls. Add the beans. Stir the dressing and pour half over them.

**5** Set the oven to 200°C, 400°F, Gas Mark 6 for the bacon and croûtons. Trim the crusts and rind from the bread and bacon, cut into squares and place on a baking tray.

**6** Slice the tomatoes and halve the slices, cutting out the hard centres of the cores. Once the potatoes are cold, arrange the tomatoes over them. Shred and add the lettuce and radicchio. Chop the parsley but do not add to the salad.

**7** Put the bread and bacon into the oven and bake for 7-10 minutes or until the croûtons are golden and the bacon crisp. Sprinkle over the salad, stir and add the rest of the dressing, and top with parsley. Serve immediately.

# · Salade Niçoise ·

Although there are a number of variations of this salad, the essential ingredients are always anchovies, eggs, olives, and tomatoes, but tuna fish, lettuce, green or yellow pepper and French or French-type beans are frequently added.

Use black olives, which in general are milder than green, and preferably those which are less highly salted (they are usually sold preserved in brine).

When served in restaurants, tuna in oil tends to be used, sometimes with so much oil that the result is more like oil soup than salad. It also drowns the garlic dressing. Here tuna in brine is used; drain off the brine and surplus anchovy oil. *For* 4.

## · INGREDIENTS ·

| | |
|---|---|
| 4-6 oz/125-190 g dwarf, Kenya or other non-string beans | 4 eggs |
| | Salt |
| ½ a Cos or other crisp lettuce | 7 oz/200 g can tuna fish in brine |
| 1 lb/500 g tomatoes (ideally, the large, sharp Provençal variety: make sure that ordinary ones are really firm) | 1½ oz/50 g can anchovy fillets |
| | Garlic Dressing (see page 95) |
| 1 green or yellow pepper | |

## • METHOD •

**1** Top and tail and wash the beans. Wash the lettuce, tomatoes, and pepper and leave to drain.

**2** Boil the eggs for 12 minutes. Meanwhile, cook the beans in boiling salted water for 5-8 minutes, until tender but still crisp. Cool the eggs with cold water and peel.

**3** Line 4 individual bowls with whole or shredded lettuce leaves. Slice the eggs and tomatoes, removing hard tomato cores, and place on top; add the tuna and beans. Halve the anchovy fillets and arrange on top. Chop the stalk end and core from the pepper and cut into rings, trimming off the white inner flesh and removing any seeds. Arrange the pepper rings and olives over the top of the salad. Stir the dressing and pour it over the salad.

# • BEAN AND FENNEL • SALAD

The beans and other ingredients in this salad act as a foil to the crispness and potency of the fennel (mild cheese could replace eggs — there is no point in using a strong variety because its flavour would be overcome).

Although fennel is not especially cheap, with English beans (which you will find in season in late summer) the rest of the salad costs relatively little.

If possible, use waxy potatoes, e.g. Maris Bard, Piper, Desirée or Pentland Crown. *For 4.*

## • INGREDIENTS •

| | |
|---|---|
| *4 oz/125 g spinach or sea-kale beet* | *8 oz/250 g dwarf or other non-string beans* |
| *1 lb/500 g new potatoes* | |
| *Salt* | *French Dressing (see page 94)* |
| *4 eggs* | *1 large or 2 small bulbs fennel* |

# • METHOD •

**1** Tear off the stalks from the spinach (or cut stems from beet) and wash. Leave to drain.

**2** Scrub the potatoes, removing green patches, and cook in boiling salted water for 15-20 minutes. Boil the eggs for 12 minutes. Wash and top and tail the beans and cook in boiling salted water for 5-8 minutes, until just tender.

**3** While still hot, slice the eggs and potatoes and chop the beans into shortish lengths and put into a salad bowl. Shred the spinach and add to the bowl. Cover with the dressing and leave while the cooked ingredients cool.

**4** Chop the top and bottom from the fennel and remove the outer layer if brownish or fibrous. Slice and wash. Dice or cut into strips and toss into the salad just before serving, reserving a little to scatter over the top.

# · BREAD ·

$B$READ REQUIRES very little time in terms of work but needs to take its own time while the yeast acts: even for rolls, which are quicker to bake than loaves (hence the tradition of fresh rolls for breakfast), a total of at least 3 hours must be allowed between mixing the dough and taking it from the oven. If fresh yeast is used, an extra 20 minutes is required at the beginning. Leave the dough to rise in a boiler-room, hot bathroom, or similar warm place, or in a sunny window in the summer.

The need for warmth arises because yeast is a living organism which raises the dough by producing carbon dioxide during respiration: light bread therefore depends on providing it with favourable growing conditions — the moistened flour supplying it with food, and its rate of growth being governed by temperature. When cold, the cells remain dormant; sudden draughts or too much heat kill them (the heat of the oven as the bread bakes destroys them all). Thus an opened door (in winter), cold or positively hot water for mixing, or the hot sides or base of a bowl put to warm in or on the cooker will impede or prevent rising: constant, all-round warmth is needed. The exact degree matters only in terms of time — which has its advantage as well as disadvantage, since in a not-so-warm place the dough can be left for a conveniently long period, e.g. all afternoon or all night (for anyone with freezing-space available, the dough can also be frozen, in which case a period of at least 4 hours should be allowed for defrosting).

'Hard' bread flour, which contains a higher proportion of gluten than ordinary 'soft' flour, makes better textured bread than the latter — and is to a varying extent more expensive. Obviously, the flour used will also govern flavour.

Fresh yeast (which looks like putty) requires activating by mixing with warm water and a little sugar before being added to the flour. The most convenient form of yeast available is dried (easy blend) which is simply sprinkled into the flour and starts working at once.

In the following recipes, a little fat or oil is usually included to prevent the bread from going stale very rapidly — like French baguettes, which, delicious as they are at breakfast-time, have become tough and dry by the evening. There is no recipe for French bread in this chapter because it is impossible to make without the appropriate flour or bakers' oven. With the addition of fat, loaves will stay reasonably fresh for 2 or 3 days and rolls for at least 12 hours. The kind of fat or oil used will affect both taste and texture: the most discreet in terms of taste is sunflower margarine, but oil has been recommended where it will complement the flavour.

# · WHITE, BROWN AND · WHOLEMEAL BREAD

Brown bread can be made with any proportion of wholemeal or other brown flour and white: two-thirds of wholemeal to one- of white, however, rises more quickly than wholemeal alone and yields bread of excellent texture.

If wholemeal alone is used, it is wise to allow at least 30 minutes' extra rising time; the dough will also be relatively slow to show obvious signs that the yeast is working during kneading, e.g. feeling springy and emitting a whooshing sound as air is pressed out (on the other hand, it is much firmer and pleasanter to handle than white).

The idea of using brine to give a crisp crust comes from *Cranks Breads and Teacakes* (compiled by Daphne Swann). *For one large loaf, two small loaves, or about 24 rolls.*

## • INGREDIENTS •

| | |
|---|---|
| ½ oz/15 g fresh yeast plus 1 teaspoon caster or soft brown sugar or 1 sachet easy blend yeast | 1 dessertpoon finely ground salt |
| | ½ oz/15 g full-fat margarine |
| ¾ pint/450 ml warm water | A little extra flour |
| 1½ lb/750 g white or wholemeal bread flour or 1 lb/500 g wholemeal plus 8 oz/250 g white | Poppy seeds or cracked wheat, to decorate (optional) |

**BRINE**

| | |
|---|---|
| 2 teaspoons finely ground salt | 2 tablespoons water |
| **One 2 lb or two 1 lb loaf tins or a baking sheet** | **Large mixing bowl** |

## • METHOD •

**1** If *using fresh yeast*: stir the yeast and sugar into ⅛ pint/80 ml of the water. The water should feel warm to the touch but not hot. Put in a warm place for 20 minutes or until frothing and creamy. Mix the flour(s) and salt in a large bowl and rub or stir in the margarine until it has disappeared (there is not enough for it to be distributed evenly throughout the flour, but this is rectified by kneading). Make a well in the middle and pour in the yeast and the rest of the water.

**2** If *using easy blend yeast*: blend the flour(s), salt, and margarine as above. Stir in the yeast, make a well, and pour in the water.

**3** Mix to a dough. At this stage, not all the flour will be taken up, but by the end of kneading most, if not the whole quantity, will be incorporated (flours vary slightly in absorbency). Knead vigorously for 5 minutes. Treat the dough like dirty washing, pummelling and pressing it down to the bottom of the bowl; if it seems easier, divide and work it in 2 or 3 lumps for part of the time. The aim is to disseminate the yeast; the warmth of one's hands also helps the yeast to act. It does not matter how much the dough is handled — the more the better (a bonus is that, if carried out at working-surface height, kneading noticeably benefits the stomach muscles). With white or partly white flour the escape of gas can be heard almost immediately. If the dough is sticky, work in extra flour; if much dry flour remains after kneading, spoon or tip it out or transfer the dough to another bowl.

**4** Cover with plastic wrap and leave to rise in a warm atmosphere for 2 hours or until it has doubled in size.

**5** Lightly grease a bread tin or tins or baking tray. 'Knock back' by kneading again for 2 minutes. A tidy way of shaping loaves not baked in a tin is plaiting; set rolls well apart to allow for rerising. Shape and place in or on the baking tin(s) or tray, cover as before, and return to a warm place to 'prove' for 25 minutes or until the dough has doubled in size a second time. Set the oven to 230°C, 450°F, Gas Mark 8.

**6** To make the brine, heat the salt and water until the salt has melted (there is no need to boil it).

**7** Paint the dough with the brine and sprinkle white dough with poppy seeds, brown with cracked wheat. Bake a large loaf for 35 minutes, smaller ones for 30 minutes and rolls for 20 minutes. Turn out the loaves and leave to cool on a wire rack.

*To freeze the dough*: put in a covered plastic container after it has been knocked back. When ready to use, remove from the freezer and leave to defrost: it is defrosted when the yeast is reactivated and it starts to rise. Knock it back a second time, shape, and proceed as above. It may seem softer than fresh dough but if defrosted thoroughly will make excellent bread.

# SUNFLOWER AND
# · SESAME SEED BREAD ·

Wheat grains and/or poppy seeds can be used for decoration. *For 1 loaf or 16-20 rolls.*

## · INGREDIENTS ·

| | |
|---|---|
| ½ oz/15 g fresh yeast plus 1 teaspoon soft brown sugar or 1 sachet easy blend yeast | ½ pint/300 ml warm water |
| | 10 oz/310 g white bread flour |

| | |
|---|---|
| 6 oz/190 g granary flour | 1 oz/25 g sunflower seeds |
| 2 teaspoons finely ground salt | 1 tablespoon sunflower oil |
| 2 teaspoons soft brown sugar | Extra flour |
| ½ oz/15 g each sesame and poppy seeds | Brine (see page 112) |
| 1 oz/25 g wholewheat grains | Wheat grains and/or poppy seeds, to decorate |
| 1 oz/25 g malted wheat flakes | **Baking sheet** |

## • METHOD •

**1** If *using fresh yeast*: stir the yeast and 1 teaspoon sugar into ⅛ pint/80 ml of the water and leave in a warm place for 20 minutes or until the yeast is frothing and creamy. Mix together the flours, salt, sugar, seeds, and wheat grains and flakes in a large bowl. Make a well in the centre and pour in the yeast. Add the remaining water and the oil.

**2** If *using easy blend yeast*: blend all the dry ingredients as above; mix in the yeast, make a well, and pour in the water. Add the oil.

**3** Work into a dough, adding more flour if needed. Cover and leave to rise for 2 hours or until doubled in size.

**4** Grease the baking sheet. Knead the dough for 2 minutes and shape into a plaited loaf or rolls: this gives a larger, better sloped surface than a plain shape for a generous grain and seed covering. Leave to prove for 25 minutes or until again doubled in size. Set the oven to 230°C, 450°F, Gas Mark 8.

**5** Paint the dough with the brine, scatter with the extra wheat and/or poppy seeds and bake the loaf for 35 minutes, rolls for 20-25 minutes.

# • CHEESE BREAD •

This is almost a meal in itself and an ideal accompaniment to vegetable dishes such as Mushroom Soup, Ratatouille, or Bean and Fennel Salad (see pages 17, 61 and 108).

Oil is included because, rather as with French bread (and despite the fat in the cheese), the fact that the latter is also salty otherwise causes the crust to lose its crispness very quickly.

The proportion of brown to white flour given produces a light-textured, golden-coloured loaf with a strong cheesy flavour; more brown or wholemeal alone will blunt the taste of the cheese somewhat but is nevertheless good in its own way. This recipe is particularly recommended for making rolls. For 1 *loaf or 12-16 rolls.*

## ▪ INGREDIENTS ▪

| | |
|---|---|
| ½ oz/15 g fresh yeast plus 1 teaspoon soft brown sugar or 1 sachet easy blend yeast | Slightly less than ½ pint/300 ml warm water |
| 8 oz/250 g strong Cheddar cheese | 2 teaspoons French mustard |
| 10 oz/310 g white bread flour | 1 tablespoon olive oil |
| 6 oz/190 g wholemeal flour | Extra flour |
| 2 teaspoons sea salt | **Baking sheet or 2 lb/1 kg bread tin** |
| Generous sprinkling of black pepper | |

## ▪ METHOD ▪

**1** *If using fresh yeast*: stir the sugar and yeast with ⅛ pint/80 ml of the water and leave in a warm place for 20 minutes or until frothy. Coarsely grate the cheese and blend 6 oz/190 g of it with the flour(s), salt, and pepper. Mix the mustard and oil with enough water to make up ⅜ pint/230 ml. Make a well in the dry ingredients and pour in the yeast and the mustard mixture.

**2** *If using easy blend yeast*: grate the cheese and mix 6 oz/190 g with the flour(s), salt, and pepper. Blend in the yeast and make a well. Stir together the mustard, oil, and enough water to make up ½ pint/300 ml and pour in.

**3** Work the mixture into a dough and knead for 5 minutes, adding extra flour if necessary. Cover and leave to rise 2 hours or until doubled in size.

**4** Grease the baking tin or sheet. Knead the dough for 2 minutes and form into a loaf or rolls, placing rolls well apart on the baking sheet. Leave to prove for 25 minutes or until again doubled in size. Set the oven to 220°C, 425°F, Gas Mark 7.

**5** Sprinkle the bread with the remaining cheese and bake a loaf for 30 minutes, rolls for 20-25 minutes.

# · WALNUT BREAD ·

The walnuts seem to enhance the flavour of the flour so that the bread tastes not only of walnut but more than usual of bread. It is not sweet and will go with almost anything — though it does not really need an accompaniment. *For 1 loaf.*

## · INGREDIENTS ·

| | |
|---|---|
| *½ oz/15 g fresh yeast plus 1 teaspoon soft brown sugar or 1 sachet easy blend yeast* | *4 oz/125 g granary flour* |
| | *2 teaspoons finely ground sea salt* |
| *½ pint/300 ml warm water* | *1 tablespoon sunflower oil* |
| *3½ oz/100 g walnut halves or pieces* | *Extra flour* |
| | Brine (*see page* 112) |
| *8 oz/250 g white bread flour* | **Baking sheet or 2 lb/1 kg bread tin** |
| *4 oz/125 g wholemeal flour* | |

## · METHOD ·

**1** *If using fresh yeast:* stir the yeast and sugar into ⅛ pint/80 ml of the water and leave in a warm place for 20 minutes or until frothing and creamy. Roughly chop the walnuts and mix with the flours and salt, make a well in the middle and pour in the yeast with the rest of the water and oil.

**2** *If using easy blend yeast:* roughly chop walnuts and mix with the flours and salt. Mix in the yeast, make a well and pour in the water and oil.

**3** Form into a dough and knead for 5 minutes, adding extra flour if necessary to counteract stickiness. Cover with plastic wrap and leave in a warm place for 2 hours or until doubled in size. The walnuts give the mixture a soft reddish tinge (the bread is also a more russet brown than usual).

**4** Knead for 2 minutes, shape into a loaf and put into a bread tin or on a baking sheet. Cover and leave in a warm place for 25 minutes or until again doubled in size. Set the oven to 220°C, 425°F, Gas Mark 7.

**5** Paint the loaf with brine and bake for 35 minutes.

# · APPLE BREAD ·

This recipe comes from the oldest known vegetarian cookery book, published around 1820 (*Vegetable Cookery* by Martha Brotherton). Although it contains sugar, it is hardly perceptibly sweet and goes especially well with cheese, notably Lancashire and Caerphilly (with which, since Mrs Brotherton lived in Lancashire, it was probably originally served). As it is kept moist by the sugar and apples, it stays fresh for several days without the addition of fat; similarly, glaze is not needed to give it a crisp crust. *For 1 loaf.*

## · INGREDIENTS ·

| | |
|---|---|
| *8 oz/250 g Bramleys or other strongly flavoured, easily mashed apples* | *8 oz/250 g wholemeal flour* |
| | *8 oz/250 g white bread flour* |
| *2 oz/50 g caster or soft brown sugar* | *Extra flour* |
| *½ pint/300 ml warm water* | **Baking sheet or 2 lb/1 kg bread tin** |
| *⅔ oz/20 g fresh yeast plus 1 teaspoonful caster or soft brown sugar or 1⅓ sachets easy blend yeast* | |

## · METHOD ·

**1** Peel, quarter, core, and chop the apples. Stew with the 2 oz/50 g sugar and 1 tablespoon of the water (which need not be warm) over low heat, stirring continuously, until the sugar has melted. Turn up the heat slightly and cook for 15-20 minutes or until the apple has turned to a thick, smooth purée. Leave to partly cool in the saucepan.

**2** If *using fresh yeast*: stir the yeast and sugar into ⅛ pint/80 ml of the water and leave in a warm place for 20 minutes or until frothing and creamy. Mix the flours together, make a well in the centre and pour in the yeast. Add the rest of the water and the apple, slightly warmed to bring it to the same temperature as the water if necessary.

**3** If *using easy blend yeast*: mix the flours and yeast, make a well in the middle and pour in the water. Add the warm apple.

**4** Work to a dough and knead for 5 minutes, adding enough extra flour to counteract stickiness. Cover and leave to rise in a warm place for 2 hours or until doubled in size.

**5** Grease the tin or baking sheet. Knead the dough for 2 minutes, shape into a loaf and leave to prove for 25 minutes or until once more doubled in size. Set the oven to 220°C, 425°F, Gas Mark 7.

**6.** Bake the loaf for 35-40 minutes, then cool on a wire rack to ensure all-round crispness.

# · SWEETENED BREADS ·

Sweetened breads and buns are a healthier option than cakes as they contain a much lower proportion of fat and sugar, as long as they are eaten without butter. The glazes and filling in the following recipes add a certain amount of sugar but make further embellishments unnecessary.

# · CRACKLY CARAMEL · BUN LOAF

Without the crackly glaze, this would be a conventional rich brown or wholemeal spiced fruit loaf (the smell as it cooks is like Christmas pudding). Gastronomically, it is particularly suited to wholemeal flour alone. However, as the high proportion of bran and fruit makes it slow to rise in this form, more than the usual quantity of yeast is recommended.

The caramel topping is quick and straightforward (it takes less than 5 minutes) but demands care. To be accurate in sugar-boiling, which depends on temperature rather than time, one really needs a thermometer: the right degree is easy to guess when using white sugar because colour serves as a guide, but more difficult with brown — which goes better with this recipe.

Buns (12-16) can be made instead of a loaf, if preferred.

## ▪ INGREDIENTS ▪

| | |
|---|---|
| ½ oz/15 g fresh yeast plus 1 teaspoon soft brown sugar or 1 sachet easy blend yeast; or, using only wholemeal flour, 1 oz/25 g fresh yeast plus 2 teaspoons sugar or 2 sachets easy blend yeast | 2 oz/50 g soft brown sugar |
| | 4 oz/125 g mixed fruit |
| | 2 oz/50 g raisins |
| ⅜ pint/230 ml warm water | Zest of 1 large orange and 1 large lemon |
| 8 oz/250 g each wholemeal and white bread flour or 1 lb/500 g wholemeal flour | 2 oz/50 g margarine |
| | 1 egg, size 3 |
| 1 teaspoon mixed spice | Extra flour |

### CARAMEL TOPPING

| | |
|---|---|
| 4 oz/125 g soft dark brown sugar (or white can be used) | 3 tablespoons water |
| Baking sheet or 2 lb/1 kg bread tin | Sugar thermometer |

## ▪ METHOD ▪

**1** *If using fresh yeast*: stir the yeast and 1 or 2 teaspoons sugar into ⅛ pint/80 ml of the water and leave in a warm place for 20 minutes or until frothy. Blend the flour(s) with the spice, 2 oz/50 g sugar, and the fruit. Wash the orange and lemon, finely grate in the zest, and mix (it tends to cling together but will be separated during kneading). Rub or stir in the margarine. Make a well and add the yeast liquid and the remainder of the water; break in the egg.

**2** *If using easy blend yeast*: mix together the flours, spice, sugar, fruit, orange and lemon zest, and margarine as above; stir in the yeast. Make a well, add the water, then break in the egg.

**3** Work into a dough and knead for 5 minutes, adding extra flour if too sticky. Cover and leave in a warm place for 2 hours or until doubled in size.

**4** Grease the tin or baking sheet. Knead the dough for 2 minutes, then shape into a loaf or rolls. Place rolls on the baking sheet their own length apart. Leave to prove for 25 minutes or until again doubled in size. Set the oven to 190°C, 375°F, Gas Mark 5. Bake a loaf for 40 minutes and buns for 17-20 minutes, until well but not too browned. As soon as cool enough to handle, place on a wire rack over cooking foil (to catch the drips from the topping).

**5** To make the caramel topping, put the sugar and water in a small, heavy saucepan, bring to the boil and boil over high heat for 3 minutes without stirring (it will be a froth of bubbles). To test the temperature of brown sugar without the aid of a sugar thermometer, drop a little into a cup of cold water; if it forms a hard ball, the caramel is ready; if it forms a string or spreads in the water, it needs a little longer. At the hard-ball stage, it will also thicken and begin to smell of burning. If using white sugar, testing in water is unnecessary since it will begin to darken; boil until it is pale brown. Remove from heat immediately and spoon over the bread while still bubbling. (To clean the saucepan and spoon, simply soak in water.)

# · STICKY HONEY AND · HAZELNUT LOAF

The 'more-ishness' of this recipe is largely due to the inclusion of bananas, which are an extravagance in that they do not contribute much taste in themselves: without them, however, the bread becomes relatively resistible.

The honey glaze really is extremely sticky: if this matters, omit it (boiling it for long enough to set it, as for caramel, will spoil the taste). To my mind though, you will not achieve the full eating experience without licking your fingers afterwards. *For 1 loaf.*

## ▪ INGREDIENTS ▪

| | |
|---|---|
| ½ oz/15 g fresh yeast plus 1 teaspoon soft brown sugar or 1 sachet easy blend yeast | 3½ oz/100 g hazelnuts (with skins) |
| 3 tablespoons water | 2 medium bananas (if large ones are used, more extra flour will be needed) |
| 12 oz/375 g granary flour | 2 tablespoons honey |
| 4 oz/125 g white bread flour | Extra flour |
| 2 oz/50 g margarine | |

### GLAZE

| | |
|---|---|
| 2 tablespoons honey | 2 tablespoons water |

**Baking sheet or 2 lb/1 kg bread tin**

## ▪ METHOD ▪

**1** If *using fresh yeast*: mix the yeast and sugar with 2 tablespoons of the water and leave in a warm place for 20 minutes or until frothy. Blend the flours and rub in the margarine. Roughly chop or pound the nuts then stir into the mixture; make a well. Mash the bananas. Warm the honey over gentle heat with the remaining tablespoon of water and stir in the banana. Check that the mixture is lukewarm, then pour into the well. Add the yeast.

**2** If *using easy blend yeast*: mix the flours and roughly chopped or pounded nuts and rub in the margarine. Mash the bananas. Warm the honey with the 3 tablespoons of water and stir in the banana. Mix the yeast into the flour and nuts, then make a well. Check that the temperature of the banana and honey is lukewarm, and pour it in.

**3** Work into a dough and knead for 5 minutes. More flour may be needed as the banana is amalgamated and liquifies: add gradually and sparingly. Cover and leave to rise in a warm place until doubled in size.

**4** Grease the tin or baking sheet. Knead the dough for 2 minutes, shape into a loaf, cover, and return to a warm place for 25 minutes or until again doubled in size. Set the oven to 190°C, 375°F, Gas Mark 5. Bake for 20 minutes; lower the oven to 180°C, 350°F, Gas Mark 4 and bake for 10 minutes more or until well browned. Place on a wire rack with cooking foil underneath to catch drips from the glaze.

**5** To make the glaze, stir the honey and water together, bring to the boil, and boil over high heat for 2½ minutes. Spoon on to the loaf and, if all-round stickiness is acceptable, spread over both the top and sides.

# TOASTED ALMOND
# · AND ORANGE ROLL ·

This recipe is designed to appeal to almond-croissant addicts. More brown flour can be used, but a nearly white dough is recommended as a contrast to the rich, dark brown frangipane filling. Rising will take only 1-1½ hours. *For 1 roll.*

## · INGREDIENTS ·

| | |
|---|---|
| ½ oz/15 g fresh yeast plus 1 teaspoon caster sugar or 1 sachet easy blend yeast | 2 oz/50 g caster sugar |
| | Zest of 1 large orange |
| ½ pint/300 ml warm water | 2 oz/50 g margarine |
| 13 oz/410 g white bread flour | Extra flour |
| 4 oz/125 g wholemeal flour | |

## FILLING

| | |
|---|---|
| 3½ oz/100 g ground almonds | 1 oz/25 g butter |
| 4 oz/125 g dark brown sugar | 1 lemon |

## GLAZE AND TOPPING

| | |
|---|---|
| 2 tablespoons orange marmalade | 1 oz/25 g almond flakes |
| **Baking sheet** | **Rolling pin** |

## • METHOD •

**1** If using fresh yeast: stir the yeast and the teaspoon of sugar into ⅛ pint/80 ml of the water and leave in a warm place for 20 minutes or until frothy. Blend the flours and 2 oz/50 g sugar; wash the orange, finely grate and mix in the zest and rub in the margarine. Make a well and pour in the yeast.

**2** If using easy blend yeast: mix the flours, sugar, orange zest, and margarine as above; stir in the yeast, make a well and pour in the water.

**3** Work into a dough and knead for 5 minutes, adding extra flour if necessary to counteract stickiness. Cover and leave to rise for 1-1½ hours or until doubled in size.

**4** To make the filling, blend the almonds and sugar. Melt the butter over gentle heat until just liquified and add to the almond mixture. Squeeze and add the juice of half the lemon. Mix well, then squeeze the other half of the lemon, and add sufficient juice to make a paste of spreadable but not runny consistency.

**5** Grease the baking sheet and flour the rolling pin and work surface. Knock back the dough and roll into an oblong about ⅓ inch/1 cm thick. Spread evenly with the filling, stopping about ½ inch/1.5 cm from the edges. Roll up from the short side like a Swiss roll and seal the ends by damping at the bottom and tucking under; similarly, damp the underside of the join on top. Place on the baking sheet, cover, and return to a warm place to prove for 20 minutes or until again doubled in size. Set the oven to 200°C, 400°F, Gas Mark 6.

**6** When proved, the roll will look like a huge Cornish pasty. Bake for 30 minutes; remove from the oven, spread with the marmalade, and sprinkle with the almonds. Bake for a further 8-10 minutes, until the almonds are toasted pale brown.

# · PIZZA NAPOLEONI ·

Although pizza originated in Naples, the name comes from an Italian novelist, Loretta Napoleoni, who gave me these recipes — which are for the classic Neapolitan type of pizza with a very thin, crisp base rather than the more solid, tart-like Anglicized version. There is a choice of four different toppings.

A practical advantage of this sort of pizza is that it takes only 8 or 9 minutes to cook, but as the topping has to be prepared as well as the dough it does not represent a quick meal unless both are ready, or partly ready, in advance.

The following quantities are for 4, but since not many people are likely to have suitable individual baking trays, they are intended for one large pizza, which fits an average full-sized 12 inch/30 cm square tray.

White and/or wholemeal flour can be used; for swift rising, choose white, but otherwise half and half is recommended. As only 12 oz/375 g flour is needed but the usual amount of yeast given, rising is proportionately quicker than for bread, about 1½ hours in a suitably warm place. *For 4.*

## · INGREDIENTS ·
### PIZZA DOUGH

| | |
|---|---|
| *½ oz/15 g fresh yeast plus 1 teaspoon caster or soft brown sugar or 1 sachet easy blend yeast* | *1 tablespoon oil* |
| *⅜ pint/230 ml warm water* | *Extra flour* |
| *6 oz/190 g wholemeal flour* | **12 inch/30 cm square (or similar-sized) baking sheet** |
| *6 oz/190 g white bread flour* | **Rolling pin** |
| *2 teaspoons salt* | |

## · METHOD ·

1 *If using fresh yeast:* stir the yeast and sugar into ⅛ pint/80 ml of the water and leave in a warm place for 20 minutes or until

frothy. Mix the flours and salt, make a well in the middle and pour in the yeast and the rest of the water; add the oil.

**2** If *using easy blend yeast*: mix the flours, salt and yeast. Make a well, pour in the water and add the oil.

**3.** Work into dough. Knead for 5 minutes, adding more flour if necessary, then cover and leave to rise for 1½ hours or until doubled in size. (The sauce for the first three toppings can be made during this time, or the spinach cooked for the fourth topping.)

**4.** Instead of knocking back as for bread, pinch and pull the dough as far as it will stretch for at least 5 minutes to give it elasticity. Cover the baking sheet with foil (dull side up) and flour the rolling pin and a suitably large surface. Roll a circle (or other shape) a little larger than the baking sheet: this will mean that the dough is no thicker than a plate. Place on the baking sheet, trim to fit, then leave to prove for 15 minutes. Set the oven to 230°C, 450°F, Gas Mark 8. It is important not to start baking the base until the oven is fully heated.

## • NAPOLITANA •

This pizza is usually, although not always, served with a finish of mozzarella cheese. The amount needed really depends on your taste: if you do not mind a less creamy result, you can get away with using a smaller amount of cheese by roughly dicing instead of slicing it and sprinkling 1½ oz/40 g of Parmesan underneath. Mozzarella cheese is sometimes sold grated; this, however, is not a good idea because, instead of being soft and moist, it becomes dry (the solid cheese is packed in whey and needs draining before use).

Use black rather than green olives (green are picked before they are fully ripe, and sharper).

### • INGREDIENTS •

| | |
|---|---|
| 1½ lb/750 g ripe tomatoes | 2-3 cloves garlic |
| Small bunch parsley (enough for 1 heaped tablespoon when chopped) | 1 tablespoon oil, preferably olive |

| | |
|---|---|
| 2 teaspoons dried oregano | 6-8 oz/190-250 g mozzarella cheese |
| Salt and pepper | 3-4 oz/90-125 g black olives |
| 1½ tablespoons tomato paste | (3 oz/90 g will be enough if the olives are small) |
| Extra oil | |
| 1½ oz/50 g can anchovy fillets | |

## • METHOD •

**1** Skin and chop the tomatoes, discarding the cores; peel and chop the garlic; wash, shake dry, and finely chop the parsley.
**2** Fry the garlic in the oil over moderate heat for 1-2 minutes, until starting to change colour. Add the oregano and tomatoes, lower the heat, season with a little salt and more pepper, and simmer for 10 minutes, crushing the tomato flesh against the sides and bottom of the pan to yield a smooth sauce. Add the tomato paste and parsley and simmer for 12 minutes or until the sauce is almost as thick as paste (which it has to be if it is not to drop off the edges of the pizza). The topping is now ready for use or can be left overnight, covered, in the refrigerator.
**3** Brush the proved dough with the extra oil, then spread evenly with the sauce. Snip the anchovy fillets in half and arrange over the top. Bake for 7 minutes. Meanwhile, drain and slice (or dice) the mozzarella cheese.
**4** Remove the pizza from the oven, shutting the door so that the temperature does not drop. Arrange the cheese and olives over the top, return to the oven, and bake for 2 minutes more, or until the cheese is just melting. Serve immediately.

## • MARGHERITA •

Substitute a small handful of roughly chopped basil leaves for the anchovies and olives. Sprinkle over the sauce before adding the cheese.

126

# · MARINARA ·

As Napolitana but omit the cheese and substitute garlic for the olives: make the sauce without (and without oil if desired), and sprinkle 6-8 chopped cloves of garlic over the top. Drizzle with about 1 tablespoon of oil and bake 8-9 minutes.

# · SPINACH ·

Traditionally, this pizza was baked as a pie, with dough on the top as well as bottom. However, this is rather solid, so the following is an adaptation. (For anyone who cares to try it as a pie, make double the quantity of dough and add both filling and the top crust before baking: prick the crust all over with a fork to ensure that it is crisp, brush with oil after baking for 5 minutes, and cook for a further 4-5 minutes.)

## · INGREDIENTS ·

| | |
|---|---|
| 1 lb/500 g spinach or sea-kale beet (but preferably spinach) | 1 large red pepper |
| Salt and pepper | 5-6 cloves garlic |
| 8 oz/250 g mozzarella cheese | 2 tablespoons oil, preferably olive |
| 1½ oz/40 g (generous 1½ tablespoons) grated Parmesan cheese | **Large saucepan with a lid** |

## · METHOD ·

1 Pick over the spinach (with beet, also cut out the stems) and wash, twice if necessary. Pack into the saucepan with ¼ teaspoon salt and 2 tablespoons water (with beet, cover the bottom of the pan with about 2 inches/5 cm) and cook over moderate heat for 6-7 minutes until submerged with liquid and tender (beet will take 10-12 minutes). Drain, press out surplus liquid, and chop. If being prepared in advance, leave to cool, cover, and put into the refrigerator.

**2** Drain and slice the mozzarella cheese and coarsely grate the Parmesan, if necessary. Wash, quarter, and dice the pepper, trimming away the white inner membrane and any mouldy spots and the seeds; peel and chop the garlic. Check the oven heat.
**3** Start cooking the pepper and garlic directly the proved dough is in the oven. Fry in the oil over moderate heat for 3-5 minutes, turning constantly, until the garlic is pale brown and the pepper softened and darkening. Add the spinach, toss to coat with oil, then lower the heat, season with a little pepper and warm gently until the dough has baked for 7 minutes. Remove the dough from the oven; because baked without a topping, it may have risen in bubbles but most of these will flatten when the spinach is added. Spread evenly with the spinach mixture, sprinkle with the Parmesan, and scatter the mozzarella over the top. Return to the oven and bake for 2 minutes more or until the cheeses have melted into each other.

# · CAKES AND TARTS ·

Cakes are eaten for pleasure, not because they are good for one: all the same, several low-fat options have been included for anyone worried about their weight. Also, nearly all the recipes contain nuts — which admittedly adds to expense but is money well spent from the nutritional point of view. I have not, however, made any attempt to introduce substitutes for sugar, since alternatives, such as fruit juice or honey, are expensive and just as fattening and bad for the teeth.

As cakes are particularly affected, it seems worth repeating the advice given about cooking with inaccurate ovens in the introduction: if one suspects that the heat is higher than it is supposed to be, allow a few minutes less cooking time (or use a marginally lower setting); to reduce the risk of burning, do not put items at the top (which, except in those which are fan-assisted, is hotter than lower down); to remedy burning at the back, turn them two or three times during cooking.

## · WALNUT AND COFFEE · CAKE

This is a moderately light, not too sweet cake which can be served without the filling and icing, if preferred.

White flour is recommended for this cake, brown destroys its character by making it rather too solid and dulling the taste of the coffee.

## ▪ INGREDIENTS ▪

| | |
|---|---|
| 8 oz/250 g walnut pieces | Salt |
| 8 oz/250 g caster sugar | 10 oz/310 g white self-raising flour |
| 8 oz/250 g margarine | 3 tablespoons strong (made) coffee |
| 4 eggs, size 2 | About ¼ pint/150 ml milk |

### FILLING

| | |
|---|---|
| 1 dessertspoon strong (made) coffee | 4 oz/125 g margarine |
| 3 oz/90 g icing sugar | |

### ICING AND DECORATION

| | |
|---|---|
| 12 oz/375 g icing sugar | Walnut halves or roughly chopped walnut pieces |
| 2 tablespoons strong (made) coffee | |
| 8 inch/20 cm cake tin | Sharp knife |

## ▪ METHOD ▪

**1** Roughly chop or crush the walnut pieces. Set the oven to 180°C, 350°F, Gas Mark 4. Line the bottom of the cake tin with cooking foil (this helps to prevent the mixture, which is relatively runny, from leaking round the sides). Grease the tin lightly, including the foil.

**2** Stir the sugar and margarine to a cream. Add the eggs and beat until smooth.

**3** Mix a pinch of salt with the flour and stir into the egg mixture. Stir in the walnuts, then the coffee. Add enough milk to bring the mixture to the consistency of thick cream: it should drop (but not drip) easily from the spoon (it may not be necessary to add quite as much as ¼ pint/150 ml). Bake for 45 minutes or until the top is firm and a skewer or knife inserted into the centre comes out clean. Leave in the tin to cool, if possible turned upside down on a wire rack.

**4** To make the filling, beat the coffee, sugar and margarine to a smooth cream. Use a sharp knife to slice the cake horizontally and lift off the top half carefully. Use the filling to sandwich the halves together.

**5** To make the icing, sieve the icing sugar into a bowl and mix with the coffee. It should be as stiff as dough: if runnier, add more sugar, otherwise it will drip down the sides of the cake. Spread smooth with a knife dipped in very hot water and decorate immediately, before the icing starts to set. Arrange walnut halves round the edge or scatter with walnut pieces.

# · POPPY SEED AND · BANANA CAKE

There are three variations of this cake – all equally popular.

The filling is made with skim-milk cheese, which, without the moist banana, tends to dry out and separate within 24 hours.

## · INGREDIENTS ·

| | |
|---|---|
| 2 largish bananas | 6 oz/190 g margarine |
| ½ oz/15 g (1 level tablespoon) poppy seeds | 6 oz/190 g white self-raising flour |
| 4 oz/125 g walnuts or walnut pieces | 3 eggs, size 2 or 3 |
| 2 oz/50 g hazelnuts | 1 lemon |
| 6 oz/190 g soft brown sugar | ½ teaspoon ground cinnamon |

### BANANA FILLING (optional)

| | |
|---|---|
| 2 small bananas | 2 oz/50 g icing sugar |
| 3½ oz/100 g Quark | **8 inch/20 cm cake tin** |

## · METHOD ·

**1** Roughly chop or crush the nuts, leaving a few still in quite large pieces.

**2** Set the oven to 180°C, 350°F, Gas Mark 4. Lightly grease the cake tin. Cream the sugar and margarine, add the eggs, and beat until smooth.

**3** Wash the lemon and finely grate the peel into the mixture. Mash and stir in the bananas (do not mash them in advance, as they turn brown on exposure to air).

**4** Mix the poppy seeds, cinnamon and nuts with the flour and add to the mixture; stir thoroughly. Transfer to the cake tin and bake for 20 minutes. Lower the oven to 150°C, 300°C, Gas Mark 2, and continue baking for another 50 minutes or until well browned and a knife or fine skewer inserted into the centre comes out clean. Leave the cake on a wire rack to become completely cold before filling.

**5** Using a sharp knife to cut the cake horizontally, lift off the top half carefully. For the filling, mash the bananas and beat in the cheese and sugar with a fork; use to sandwich the two halves.

## · ORANGE AND BANANA CAKE ·

Substitute the finely grated peel of 1 large orange and a squeeze of lemon juice for the poppy-seed and lemon zest.

## · GINGER AND BANANA CAKE ·

Add about a ¾ inch/2 cm length of root ginger, coarsely grated, to Orange and Banana Cake.

# · VERY RICH FRUIT CAKE ·

I admit that as it stands this is expensive — but it carries the bonus that it really is filling: also, so long as one sticks to the proportions of basic ingredients, i.e. fat, sugar, eggs, and flour, one can subtract (or add) to the amounts of fruit and nuts more or less to convenience. Brandy ensures that it will keep but is by no means essential.

## • INGREDIENTS •

| | |
|---|---|
| 3½ oz/100 g walnuts or walnut pieces | 4 oz/125 g plain or self-raising white flour |
| 3½ oz/100 g hazelnuts or almonds (preferably with skins) | Pinch salt |
| | 1 level teaspoon mixed spice |
| 8 oz/250 g soft dark brown sugar | 8 oz/250 g mixed fruit |
| 8 oz/250 g soft margarine | 8 oz/250 g raisins |
| 4 eggs, size 2 or 3 | Finely grated zest of 1 orange |
| 1 tablespoon brandy (optional) | **8 inch/20 cm cake tin** |
| 4 oz/125 g wholemeal flour | |

## • METHOD •

**1** Set the oven to 120°C, 250°F, Gas Mark ½. Grease the cake tin. Roughly chop the nuts. Cream the sugar and margarine; add the eggs and beat until smooth. Stir in the brandy, if using.

**2** Mix the flours, salt, and spice and stir in; add the fruit and nuts, separating any fruit which has stuck together, and the orange zest. Stir vigorously, turn into the tin and bake for 1 hour 35 minutes or until the cake is evenly brown and a knife or fine skewer stuck into the centre comes out clean.

# • FATLESS FRUIT CAKE •

This recipe is similar to tea bread but does not need to be eaten with butter, but could be iced with the Lemon Filling for Francatelli's Fatless Almond Cake (see page 134), if wished.

The cake takes only a few minutes to make, but 2 hours are needed for the mixture to soak before baking.

To keep, wrap in a food bag and store in the refrigerator, otherwise it quickly becomes dry.

## ▪ INGREDIENTS ▪

| | |
|---|---|
| 3½ oz/100 g walnuts or walnut pieces | ½ pint/300 ml milk |
| 1 eating apple | 6 oz/190 g white or wholemeal self-raising flour (wholemeal adds to the nutty texture) |
| 6 oz/190 g currants and raisins or mixed fruit | |
| | 1 level teaspoon bicarbonate of soda |
| 6 oz/190 g soft brown sugar | **Bread tin or 7 inch/17 cm cake tin** |
| 3 oz/90 g All-Bran | |

## ▪ METHOD ▪

**1** Roughly chop or crush the nuts. Peel and coarsely grate or finely chop the apple. Mix together all the ingredients except the flour and soda and leave for 2 hours.

**2** Set the oven to 180°C, 350°F, Gas Mark 4, and lightly grease the bread or cake tin. Stir in the flour and soda. Turn into the tin and bake for 45 minutes until a skewer inserted into the centre comes out clean. Cool on a wire rack before adding icing, if using.

# FRANCATELLI'S
# ▪ FATLESS ALMOND ▪
# CAKE

Francatelli was probably the most distinguished chef of his day and for a short time *maître d' hôtel* (head chef) to Queen Victoria (he was sacked, not because of any fault in his cooking but for losing his temper with a kitchen maid). The original recipe calls for almond essence rather than lemon juice and recommends making little cakes in paper cases; the mixture, however, can also be used for flat cakes or biscuits to accompany ices or yoghurt, or for a single large cake.

As its character comes from the contrast of the grittiness of the nuts with the soufflé-like texture of the sponge, use whole rather than ready ground almonds.

To achieve the light texture, an egg whisk is virtually essential. The following is enough for one fairly big cake or about 40 small cakes/biscuits: if you plan to make the latter, you can halve the quantity, if wished. It is worth using the whole amount for a single cake, however, since it stays fresh for a surprisingly long time. The low-fat filling made with skim-milk cheese is only suitable if the cake is eaten within 24 hours.

## ▪ INGREDIENTS ▪

| | |
|---|---|
| 4 oz/125 g whole almonds (with skins) | 8 oz/250 g caster sugar |
| | 4 oz/125 g wholemeal plain flour |
| 6 eggs, size 2 | Pinch salt |
| 2 medium lemons | |

### LEMON FILLING

| | |
|---|---|
| ½ large lemon | 4 oz/125 g icing-sugar |
| 4 oz/125 g skim-milk or medium-fat soft cheese (such as curd) | **8 inch/20 cm cake tin or cake cases and/or baking tray** |
| **Egg whisk** | |
| **2 large mixing bowls** | |

## ▪ METHOD ▪

**1** Crush the almonds fairly but not very finely, so that a few are left as small chips.

**2** Separate the egg yolks and whites. Wash the eggs in case bits of shell fall into the whites; it is also advisable to separate each one over a cup or bowl by itself so that if a whole or part of a yolk escapes the other whites are not affected. (If this happens and it cannot be removed, the egg should be used for something else, since the presence of yolk will prevent the whites from whipping satisfactorily.) Crack smartly in the middle, hold over the cup, and tip the yolk from one half of the shell to the other until all the white has fallen out. Empty the yolks into one large mixing bowl and transfer the whites to the second.

**3** Squeeze the lemons. Beat the yolks smooth and stir in the lemon juice, sugar, flour, salt and almonds.

**4** Set the oven to 180°C, 350°F, Gas Mark 4. Line a baking sheet or the bottom of the cake tin with cooking foil and grease generously; alternatively, spread cake cases on the baking tray. Add a pinch of salt to the whites and whip until they are opaque, fine-textured, and stiff enough to hold their shape when twirled or dropped from the whisk.

**5** Fold (very gently stir) the whites into the mixture containing the yolks, turning gently from the bottom upwards in a figure of eight motion until no pockets of white remain.

**6** Bake a single cake in two halves; for biscuits, place table-spoons of the mixture on to the baking sheet at least 1½ inches/ 4 cm apart to allow for spreading; half-fill cake cases. Bake biscuits for 25 minutes, little cakes for 30 minutes and cake halves for 45 minutes.

**7** The cake is delicate; you can carefully remove the first half from the tin before it is cool in order to proceed with baking the second, but leave it on the foil until completely cold. Similarly, do not remove the biscuits from the foil until cold.

**8** To make the filling, squeeze the lemon. Add the juice to the cheese and sugar and beat smooth with a fork. Sandwich the two cake halves together with the filling, or use it to ice small cakes and biscuits.

**Variation** Raspberry or other jam can be used for the filling.

# · REALLY EXTRAVAGANT ·
# CHOCOLATE CAKE

This is an extra-rich chocolate cake — known in my house as 'disaster' cake from the fact that, even among items of this sort, few are so fattening or spot-inducing: hence all the more reason to ensure that it is worth the spots. To make it truly delicious means using the best chocolate possible — which (as always) means expense. One of the best flavoured brands of cooking chocolate currently available is Menier Chocolat Patissier but other plain chocolate can be used. Do not use milk chocolate as the less pronounced flavour is lost among the other ingredients.

Besides chocolate, the cake contains a high proportion of nuts and relatively little flour, which means it will stay moist for a remarkably long time (it is almost as good after a week as when it is first made). The cake can be iced all over or just on the top — choose the appropriate set of ingredients.

## ▪ INGREDIENTS ▪

| | |
|---|---|
| 3½ oz/100 g walnut halves or pieces | 6 oz/190 g soft dark brown sugar |
| | 6 oz/190 g margarine |
| 6 oz/190 g cooking or plain chocolate | 4 eggs, size 2 |
| | 2 oz/50 g ground almonds |
| 1 tablespoon strong (made) coffee or water | 3 oz/90 g white self-raising flour |

### FILLING

| | |
|---|---|
| 1½ oz/40 g ground almonds (or the rest of 3½ oz/100 g packet left over from the cake) | 3 oz/90 g butter |
| | 2 oz/50 g cooking or plain chocolate |

### ICING FOR TOP AND SIDES

| | |
|---|---|
| 2½ oz/70 g icing sugar | 3 oz/90 g butter |
| 6 oz/190 g cooking or plain chocolate | 1 tablespoon (made) coffee or water |

### ICING FOR TOP ONLY

| | |
|---|---|
| 2½ oz/70 g icing sugar | 2 oz/50 g butter |
| 4 oz/125 g chocolate | 3 teaspoons coffee or water |

### DECORATION (OPTIONAL)

Almonds or walnut halves

**8 inch/20 cm cake tin**

## ▪ METHOD ▪

**1** Set the oven to 150°C, 300°F, Gas Mark 2; grease the cake tin. To make the cake, finely crush the walnuts with a pestle and mortar.

**2** Break the chocolate into a small saucepan and melt with the water or coffee over very low heat. Stir continuously and remove before it has completely melted; continue stirring until smooth.
**3** Stir the sugar and margarine to a cream. Beat in the eggs one by one; continue beating until the mixture is smooth (it will be fairly liquid). Stir in the melted chocolate. Add the almonds, walnuts and flour. Mix well.
**4** The cake can be cooked whole but comes out better if cooked in two halves. Pour half the mixture into the tin and bake for 30 minutes, until a skewer inserted into the centre comes out clean, then grease the tin and repeat with the second half. If baking the whole mixture, bake for 70 minutes. Remove from the tin and leave to cool on a wire rack.
**5** Meanwhile, make the filling. Chop the butter into smallish pieces and break up the chocolate. Melt in a small saucepan over very low heat until the chocolate is nearly liquified. Remove, stir smooth, then mix in the almonds. When the cake is cold, it should be stiffer than butter; if not, chill in the refrigerator.
**6** For the icing, sieve the icing sugar if it is lumpy. Break up or chop the chocolate and butter as above and put into a small saucepan with the coffee or water. Heat gently until the chocolate is nearly melted, then add the icing sugar and stir until smooth. The mixture should be stiff enough to hold its shape; if necessary, add a little extra icing sugar. Set ready a mug of very hot water, spoon the icing over the cake, and spread with a knife dipped in the water (this prevents the icing from sticking to it: dip as often as required). Decorate with walnuts or almonds.

# CHOCOLATE
# · PROFITEROLES ·

These hardly need an introduction beyond the reminder that they come into the same category as Really Extravagant Chocolate Cake (see page 136) — and in a way are worse because they are so airy and insubstantial that one ends up eating far more.

The pastry for profiteroles and éclairs (the only difference is shape) can be neatly piped with piping bags, but if the dough is made in advance and chilled in the refrigerator, it is easy to shape into balls with floured hands (the other option is to use a paper bag with a hole cut out of the corner). Except with Menier chocolate, which hardens almost immediately, several hours may also be needed for the icing to set.

The pastry can be made with white and/or brown flour but with all wholemeal is rather bread-like: a mixture, however, gives a light but more interesting result than white alone.

Whipping cream, which is thinner and cheaper than double, is suitable for a filling without added liquid but otherwise tends to curdle before sufficiently thick. Do not use very thick cream such as Jersey since it turns to butter if whipped.

As the success of the pastry depends partly on accurate proportions, precise metric equivalents are given. *Enough for about 14 buns.*

## • INGREDIENTS •

| | |
|---|---|
| 1½ oz/45 g wholemeal flour | 2 eggs, size 2 or 3 |
| 1½ oz/45 g white self-raising flour | Extra white flour for shaping the profiteroles |
| 2 oz/60 g butter | |
| ¼ pint/140 ml water | |

**FILLING**

| |
|---|
| ¼ pint/150 ml whipping cream |

**ICING**

| | |
|---|---|
| 3½ oz/100 g cooking or other plain chocolate | 1 tablespoon made coffee or water |

**Baking sheet**

## • METHOD •

1 Mix the flours together and transfer to a mug (this makes it easier to add it all at the same time). Chop up the butter and put into a small saucepan with the water. Heat gently until it has melted, then bring to the boil. When bubbling is vigorous, tip in

the flour. Turn off the heat and beat to a smooth, stiff dough. Leave for a few minutes to cool.

**2** Beat in the eggs one by one; do not add the second until the first is completely blended into the dough, with no free liquid, and so that it is almost as stiff as before. After both have been incorporated, it should have the consistency of paste or whipped cream. The dough can be shaped into balls as soon as it is cold but is much easier to handle if chilled (covered) for a few hours in the refrigerator.

**3** Set the oven to 220°C, 425°F, Gas Mark 7. Lightly grease the baking sheet and put a tablespoon of flour (white) on a saucer. Rub it over the palms of the hands and roll the dough into balls about the size of walnuts. Place on the sheet far enough apart to allow for each to quadruple; keep hands well floured and wash if they get sticky. Bake for 20 minutes, during which time do not open the oven door (sudden loss of heat may cause the buns to sink). The buns will have puffed up enormously and should be as brown as well-baked buns of bread; if still pale, cook for a further 1-2 minutes. Leave on a wire rack until completely cold before icing.

**4** To make the icing, break the chocolate into squares, put into a small saucepan with the coffee or water and heat very gently, stirring continuously, until almost melted. Remove from the heat and stir until smooth. Spoon a dollop over each profiterole and, if necessary, spread with a knife heated by dipping in very hot water. Leave to set.

**5** Do not fill the profiteroles until shortly before serving. Whip the cream until stiff. Make a slit halfway up the side of each bun and insert the cream with a teaspoon.

**Variations** Add any of the following ingredients to the cream and whip until stiff.

## · COFFEE FILLING ·

| | |
|---|---|
| ¼ pint/150 ml whipping cream | 1½ oz/40 g caster sugar |
| 2 heaped teaspoons instant coffee granules or powder | |

## · BRANDY FILLING ·

| ¼ pint/150 ml double cream | 1½ oz/40 g caster sugar |
|---|---|
| 1 tablespoon brandy | |

## ·ORANGE FILLING·

As Brandy Filling plus the finely grated zest of ½ an orange

# BROWN BREAD
# ·TREACLE TART WITH·
# LEMON

Wholemeal bread and walnut gives the filling a crunchy texture, and the lemon offsets the sweetness of the treacle.

### · INGREDIENTS ·

| 1 quantity Flaky Pastry made with cream dough (see page 40) | 2 oz/50 g walnuts or walnut pieces |
|---|---|
| | 1 oz/25 g butter |
| 4 oz/125 g stale brown bread for grating (fresh bread tends to form doughy lumps) | 1 lb/500 g golden syrup |
| | 8½ inch/22 cm tart dish |
| 1 large lemon | |

### · METHOD ·

**1** Set the oven to 180°C, 350°F, Gas Mark 4. Line the tart dish with the pastry.
**2** Coarsely grate the bread; wash and dry the lemon and grate the zest and squeeze the juice from one half. Chop walnuts.

**3** Put the butter and syrup into the saucepan and warm gently until the butter has melted.

**4** Add the breadcrumbs, lemon zest and juice, and nuts to the syrup. Mix thoroughly, then pour into the pastry case. Bake for 30 minutes. Eat cold.

# CHOCOLATE
# · MERINGUES ·

The advantage of these is that although they really do taste of chocolate the amount they contain is almost negligible (if eaten alone, without cream filling, each meringue yields only about 50 calories). The cream does not contain sugar, unlike the filling for biscuits, to provide a contrast to the sweetness of the meringues.

Although cheap (without cream filling) meringues are wasteful in that only the whites of eggs are used: the yolks, however, can be used for ice cream (but at the price of rather a lot more cream: see page 171).

It is not worth attempting this recipe without an egg whisk. *For 18-20 meringues or 9-10 pairs.*

## · INGREDIENTS ·

| | |
|---|---|
| 1 oz/25 g plain chocolate | Pinch of finely ground salt |
| 4 eggs, size 2 or 3 | 8 oz/250 g caster sugar |

### CHOCOLATE CREAM FILLING (OPTIONAL)

| | |
|---|---|
| 1½ oz/45 g plain chocolate | ¼ pint/150 ml double cream |
| 1 tablespoon water | **Baking sheet** |
| **Egg whisk** | |

## · METHOD ·

**1** Finely grate the chocolate.

**2** Separate the eggs. Wash (in case pieces of shell drop into the whites) and break each one over a cup or bowl by itself. Crack sharply in the middle and tip the yolk from one half of the shell to the other until all the white has fallen out. Transfer the whites to the large bowl.

**3** Line the baking sheet with cooking foil and grease lightly. Set the oven to 110°C, 225°F, Gas Mark ¼. Add a pinch of salt to the egg whites and whip until they are close-textured and stiff enough to hold their shape when raised on the whisk or dropped. Whisk in half the sugar. Fold (very gently stir) in the rest. Fold in the chocolate.

**4** Set heaped dessertspoonsful at least 1 inch/2.5 cm apart on the baking sheet, twirling the tops for a decorative finish. Bake for 1 hour 20 minutes (very low heat is used because the aim is merely to dry out the mixture rather than bake it). As the chocolate does not completely melt, it will produce a speckled effect. Leave to cool.

**5.** To make the filling, break the chocolate into a small saucepan and heat very gently with the water, stirring continuously, until almost melted. Stir until smooth and allow to cool. Add to the cream and whisk to a sufficiently thick consistency to hold its shape. Sandwich the meringues together with the filling.

# · QUICK CHOCOLATE · BISCUITS

These have a crisp, melt-in-the-mouth texture rather like Viennese Fancies and can similarly be sandwiched with cream, though the chocolate flavour gives them sufficient interest not really to need filling.

Cooking time is 45 minutes (slow baking helps to give them their crispness) but they can be prepared, excluding filling, in about 5 minutes. The chocolate cream filling is also quick to make. *Enough for 16-18 plain biscuits or 8-9 pairs.*

### ▪ INGREDIENTS ▪

| | |
|---|---|
| 3½ oz/100 g cooking or other plain chocolate | 4 oz/125 g margarine |

| 2 oz/50 g caster sugar | 6 oz/190 g plain white flour |
| --- | --- |

**CHOCOLATE CREAM FILLING**

| 2 oz/50 g plain chocolate | ¼ pint/150 ml double cream |
| --- | --- |
| 1 tablespoon water | 3 oz/90 g caster sugar |
| **Baking sheet** | **Egg Whisk** |

## • METHOD •

**1** Set the oven to 120°C, 250°F, Gas Mark ½. Lightly grease the baking sheet. Break the chocolate into a small saucepan with about 1 oz/25 g of the margarine and stir over low heat until it is almost melted. Remove from the heat and continue stirring while the remainder melts.

**2** Beat the sugar and the rest of the margarine to a cream. Stir in first the chocolate, then the flour. Mould into a stiff dough and roll into balls about the size of walnuts. Flatten, then place on the baking sheet 2 inches/5 cm apart to allow for spreading. Prick with a fork, and bake for 45 minutes. Leave to cool completely.

**3** To make the filling, melt the chocolate in the water over low heat until almost melted as above; allow to cool for a few minutes. Put into a bowl with the cream and sugar and whisk until stiff enough to hold its shape, then sandwich the biscuits.

# • BAKE-AS-YOU-EAT • ROCK CAKES

The idea of these is to leave a bowl of the uncooked mixture in the refrigerator and cook a few at a time whenever you feel hungry. They take 15 minutes to bake (in a preheated oven) and are better hot than cold. (They are also quick to make.)

If you want the mixture to last more than 3 days, brandy or a similar spirit is essential.

As they do not contain much sugar and are lower in fat than the standard proportion for cakes, they are relatively healthy.
Makes 14-16.

## ▪ INGREDIENTS ▪

| | |
|---|---|
| 4 oz/125 g margarine | 3 oz/90 g muesli |
| 2 oz/50 g soft brown sugar | Salt |
| 1 egg, size 2 or 3 | 4 oz/125 g raisins |
| 1 tablespoon brandy (optional) | 3½ oz/100 g each of 2 sorts of nuts (walnuts or walnut pieces, hazelnuts, Brazil or cashew nuts, almonds, peanuts) |
| Finely grated zest of 1 orange | |
| 3 oz/90 g wholemeal flour | |
| 3 oz/90 g white, preferably self-raising, flour | **Baking tray** |

## ▪ METHOD ▪

**1** If these cakes are to be eaten at once, set the oven to 200°C, 400°F, Gas Mark 6 and grease the baking tray. Beat the margarine and sugar to a cream. Stir in the egg, then the brandy, if using. Add the orange zest.

**2** Blend together the flours, muesli, and a very small pinch of salt and add to the mixture. Stir in the raisins. Roughly chop and add the nuts. Stir until the flour is amalgamated. The mixture will be just moist enough to be cohesive.

**3** Spoon heaped dessertspoonsful of the mixture on to the baking tray at least ½ inch/1.5 cm apart (an average-sized tray will not take the whole quantity at once). Bake for 15 minutes or until golden brown.

# PARTIES AND
# ·DINNER PARTIES·

IF LOTS OF people are coming to eat and a sit-down meal is impractical, my suggestions (with cost in mind) are: dip(s) or pâté(s) with bread (plenty); hot or cold quiche or tart, e.g. cold Carrot and Walnut Tart (see page 42) or the Spinach and Pine Nut Tart given in this chapter, both of which are extremely filling, plus salad and perhaps Chocolate Meringues (see page 142), a cake, or ices; invariably popular extras are Cheese Straws or hot or cold Savoury Profiteroles.

Good ideas for dinner parties are Lasagne (see page 33) and moussaka, both of which can be made ahead and do not need accompaniments. In addition, there are further suggestions, all of which can either be prepared in advance or, in the case of Chicken with Orange, do not take much time to prepare anyway.

If you want a first course, dips are again ideal (see pages 11 to 16), partly because they can be eaten communally (saves on crockery and washing-up). The Taramasalata recipe on page 147 is expensive but particularly suitable before moussaka — or serve Tsatziki; Smoked Mackerel Pâté goes well with Lamb, Kidney and Mushroom Pie, and Hummus with Chicken with Orange and Brandy. A simple salad such as Beans with Onions or Leeks with Olives (see pages 102 and 103) could precede Lasagne or Steve's Moussaka (which is vegetarian); Mushroom Soup (see page 17) would go well with Chestnut Pie or Spinach and Pine Nut Tart served as a main course; or simply serve avocado pears with French Dressing (see page 94).

For a pudding, serve Fernando's Passion Cake, Chocolate Pro-fiteroles with sauce rather than icing (see page 138); or try Hazelnut Meringue Cake (the out-and-out favourite in my house: see page 166), ices, which have the advantage that they can be made whenever is convenient and kept in the freezer, or — one of the very few really healthy pudding options — fruit salad which is extremely easy to make, and also quite cheap if you use the fruits that happen to be in season at the time.

# · TINA KARAGEORGIS'S ·
# TARAMASALATA

Tina is Kaity Karageorgis's daughter, and this is her favourite version of the Greek recipe taramasalata. The ingredients are dear but, as the flavour is strong (and the content very rich), a little is enough.

Mashed potato can be used to bind the mixture instead of bread, as I have suggested here, but it makes the preparation time considerably longer. *For about 6.*

## · INGREDIENTS ·

| | |
|---|---|
| *2 oz/50 g white bread without crust* | *1 small clove garlic* |
| *8 oz/250 g smoked cods' roe* | *Black pepper* |
| *1 large lemon* | *4-6 tablespoons olive oil* |

## · METHOD ·

**1** Soak the bread in water and wring dry. Peel the skin from the roe, pulling gently so as to remove it cleanly. Squeeze the juice from the lemon.

**2** Peel, chop and crush the garlic in a pestle and mortar. Add the bread, roe, lemon juice, and a generous sprinkling of pepper. Pound together, pouring in the oil by degrees and taking care to pulverize any hard, red layers of roe next to the skin. The amount of oil given will produce a fairly firm result; for a runnier consistency, add a little more.

# · LAMB, KIDNEY AND · MUSHROOM PIE

This substantial dish is ideal for a party because it can be made in advance and needs no last-minute attention. Serve with boiled potatoes and any other plainly cooked vegetable or Green Salad (see page 102).

Ideally, purchase and cook kidneys on the same day; otherwise buy them in their fat or check that they look plump and firm.

A little red wine will enhance the flavour but is not essential.

If possible, use a pie dish which has a broad rim on which to stick the pastry. The pie fits a medium-sized dish (8 × 11 inches/20 × 27 cm) but a larger one can be used if a small ovenware bowl of about the same depth (e.g. a ramekin dish) is placed in the middle to take the place of some of the filling. In this case, use 1½ quantities of pastry.  *For 6.*

## · INGREDIENTS ·

| | |
|---|---|
| 2½ lb/1.25 kg half leg of lamb | Salt and pepper |
| 4 lambs' kidneys | ¼ pint/150 ml water and/or red wine |
| 8 oz/250 g mushrooms, preferably large ones | 1 quantity Flaky Pastry made with cream dough (see page 40) |
| 1 medium onion | |
| 2-3 cloves garlic | **Medium-sized pie dish** |

## · METHOD ·

**1** Wash the lamb in cold or lukewarm water. With the upper half, remove the bone by simply cutting round it; with the lower, slice two or three steaks from the side which carries most of the meat and cut down the bone to remove the chunk at the end. A little meat will remain at the top which can either be trimmed off or left on the bone for soup (see page 24). Remove all the fat and chop into 1 inch/2.5 cm squares.

**2** If the kidneys are in their fat, pull it away. Make a shallow slit in each and peel off the inner skin; pull sharply where it joins the central core. Sniff to check freshness, then wash. Slice into 5 or 6 pieces, cutting out or round the core.

**3** Set the oven to 180°C, 350°F, Gas Mark 4. Peel and wipe (or wash button) mushrooms. Peel and coarsely chop the onion; peel and finely chop the garlic.

**4** Put one-third of the lamb into the pie dish and season moderately with salt and pepper; add half the kidneys and prepared vegetables. Repeat the layers, then finish with a layer of lamb. (If using a pie dish which is too large, put a bowl in the middle before starting to fill it to take up some of the space, as it is important that the contents should reach the top or the pastry will sink.) Pour in the water and/or wine.

**5** Roll out the pastry to a circle slightly larger than the pie dish. Wet the rim of the dish and put on the pastry cover. Press down the edges and trim; mend any cracks with the trimmings (wet the underside of the pastry to make it stick) and keep the rest for decoration. Press round the edges with a fork and make an air hole in the middle. Re-roll the trimmings and cut out leaves or other shapes to stick round the centre.

**6** Bake for 30 minutes, then cover loosely with cooking foil (this prevents the pastry from becoming too brown) and bake for a further 70-75 minutes. If made in advance, reheat at the same temperature, covered, for 25 minutes.

# · STEVE'S MOUSSAKA ·

Steve (a student at Durham) makes this by degrees: first he cooks the lentils and does something else while they cook; then boils the potatoes; then makes the lentil sauce; then, probably a bit later, slices and leaves the aubergines to sweat — so that, by the time they are ready to grill, the moussaka is three-quarters prepared (the method below, however, is in the order which is quickest if one is making it all at once).

Use whole green rather than split lentils and if possible choose waxy potatoes over floury ones.

Allow an hour for the aubergines to sweat. *For 4-6.*

## ▪ INGREDIENTS ▪

| | |
|---|---|
| 2 large aubergines, weighing about 1½ lb/750 g | 8 oz/250 g ripe tomatoes |
| Salt and pepper | 8 oz/250 g mushrooms (large or small) |
| 2 oz/50 g green lentils | 4-5 tablespoons oil |
| 1 lb/500 g potatoes | 1 teaspoon ground nutmeg |
| 1 large or two medium onions | 2 teaspoons dried oregano |
| 2-3 cloves garlic | 3 tablespoons tomato paste |

### BÉCHAMEL SAUCE

| | |
|---|---|
| 2 oz/50 g Parmesan cheese | 2 tablespoons oil |
| 1 pint/600 ml milk | 2 oz/50 g white flour |
| 1 oz/15 g butter | |
| **Large baking tray** | **Largish ovenware dish** |

## ▪ METHOD ▪

**1** Wash the aubergines, slice into ¼ inch/0.75 cm slices, sprinkle with fine salt, and place in a colander for 1 hour to sweat. Rinse and leave to drain.

**2** Rinse the lentils, bring to the boil in unsalted water, and boil briskly for 10 minutes. Reduce the heat and simmer for 30-35 minutes until tender; add a little salt when they are almost ready. Drain, reserving 1 tablespoon of the cooking water.

**3** Peel the potatoes and cook in boiling salted water for 15-20 minutes, until just soft. Allow to cool and slice moderately thinly.

**4** Peel and chop the onion(s), garlic, and tomatoes, discarding the tomato cores; wash or peel mushrooms, and slice.

**5** Fry the onion over low heat in 2 tablespoons of the oil, turning frequently, for 10 minutes or until soft. Add the mushrooms and garlic, season lightly with pepper and very lightly with salt, and fry for 5 minutes more. Add the tomatoes, season lightly with pepper again, and continue frying for 2-3 minutes. Remove from the heat and stir in the nutmeg, oregano, tomato paste and lentils plus the 1 tablespoon of cooking water.

**6** Grill the aubergines. Line a large plate with kitchen roll and the baking sheet with cooking foil. Spread the sheet with 1/1½ tablespoons of oil (if it has no sides, turn up the edges of the foil to prevent dripping), blot the slices on the kitchen roll to remove remaining moisture, and place as many as will fit without overlapping on the sheet (a 12 inch/30 cm square sheet will take slightly more than half). Turn so that both sides are moistened, set the grill to medium, then grill for 5-7 minutes per side until light brown in the middle (colouring tends to be uneven). Transfer to a plate and repeat with the remaining aubergines.

**7** Arrange half or one-third of the aubergines, depending on the width of the dish, over the bottom of the ovenware dish. Spread with half or one-third of the sauce and then the same amount of potato. Repeat once or twice. If to be served at once, set the oven to 200°C, 400°F, Gas Mark 6.

**8** To make the béchamel sauce, coarsely grate the cheese if necessary. Heat, but do not boil, the milk. Melt the butter in the oil over low heat, add the flour, and mix until smooth, then pour in the milk slowly, stirring continuously. Season moderately and continue stirring until the sauce is thick. Simmer for 3 minutes, remove from the heat and stir in the cheese. Pour over the moussaka and bake for 25 minutes or until the top is golden.

# · CHESTNUT PIE ·

This is not too expensive and fairly festive, with quite as interesting a flavour as any kind of meat pie (it could be enriched with about 4 oz/125 g chopped ham added with the mushrooms).

The chestnuts need soaking overnight (dried rather than fresh are recommended not only for practical reasons, notably the time needed for skinning, but because the latter do not have the same concentration of flavour). *For 4-5.*

## · INGREDIENTS ·

| | |
|---|---|
| *Double quantity Flaky Pastry made with cream (see page 40)* | *8 oz/250 g dried chestnuts, soaked in cold water overnight* |

| | |
|---|---|
| 1 *large parsnip, weighing about 8 oz/250 g* | 3 *tablespoons oil* |
| *Salt* | *Pepper* |
| 1 *medium onion* | *Large glass red wine (optional)* |
| 2-3 *cloves garlic* | 1 *level tablespoon white flour* |
| 8 *oz/250 g mushrooms* | **Pie dish or deep 8½ inch/ 22 cm tart dish** |
| 1 *red pepper* | |

## · METHOD ·

**1** Drain and pick over the chestnuts, removing any black parts and pieces of skin. Peel the parsnip and cut in half across.

**2** Put the parsnip and chestnuts in a saucepan, cover with water and season moderately with salt. Bring to the boil, then simmer for 10-15 minutes or until the parsnip is just soft all through. Remove the parsnip and simmer the chestnuts for 20 minutes more or until they too are soft. Drain but do not throw away the water. Mash roughly with a fork; cut the parsnip into medium slices.

**3** Peel and slice the onion; peel and chop the garlic; peel and wipe large or wash small mushrooms, trim the stems, and slice fairly finely; wash and cut the pepper in half, removing the seeds, white inner membrane, and any dark spots, and chop into sticks or small squares.

**4** Fry the onion in the oil over gentle heat for 10 minutes, stirring frequently; add the garlic and pepper and continue frying for 5 more minutes or until the skin of the pepper begins to darken. Add the mushrooms, season slightly with salt and pepper, and fry for 1-2 minutes.

**5** If using the red wine, make up to ½ pint/300 ml with the chestnut water. Sprinkle the flour into the pan, stir until amalgamated, then add the water and wine or ½ pint/300 ml of the water alone. Simmer gently for 3-5 minutes, stirring constantly, while the sauce thickens, then remove from the heat.

**6** Unless being made in advance, set the oven to 200°C, 400°F, Gas Mark 6. Line the dish with half the pastry, taking care to leave enough for the top. Spread half the chestnuts at the bottom and cover with half the contents of the frying pan. Add the slices of parsnip, the rest of the chestnuts, and finally the rest of the vegetables and sauce. Roll out the remaining pastry, wet the edges of the pastry lining, and cover, pressing the edges firmly together. Trim, using the remains of the pastry for decoration, press the edge with a fork, and make an air hole in the middle. To keep overnight, cover with plastic wrap and store unbaked in the refrigerator (baking and reheating tend to make it too dry). Bake for 1 hour: if the pastry becomes too coloured, cover loosely with cooking foil.

# CHESTNUT
# · CROQUETTES ·

One of the advantages of this recipe is that it can be made at the same time or instead of chestnut stuffing for turkey and is therefore convenient for mixed vegetarian and non-vegetarian Christmas dinners.

Like Chicken Maryland (see page 79), the croquettes are baked in breadcrumbs and are as crisp as if they were fried although in fact relatively low-fat.

Canned chestnuts are suggested not merely to save time but because their mushy texture gives a suitably smooth consistency. *Enough for 10 medium-sized croquettes.*

## · INGREDIENTS ·

| | |
|---|---|
| 7 oz/225 g can unsweetened whole chestnuts | Small handful parsley (enough for 1 tablespoon when chopped) |
| 3½ oz/100 g walnuts or walnut pieces | 1 teaspoon yeast extract |
| 1 stick celery | 1 oz/25 g butter |
| 1 large onion | 1 oz/25 g flour |
| 2-3 cloves garlic | 1 large egg |

| | |
|---|---|
| *3 oz/90 g (3 average slices) stale brown or white bread for breadcrumbs (fresh bread tends to form doughy lumps)* | *About 1 tablespoon oil* |
| | *Salt and pepper* |
| | **Baking tray** |

## ▪ METHOD ▪

**1** Trim the leaf and root ends from the celery, remove any brown patches, then wash, and finely chop. Wash, shake or pat dry, and chop the parsley; peel and finely chop the onion and garlic. Roughly crush the walnuts; drain the chestnuts, keeping the liquor, and mash. Chop the butter into small pieces.

**2** Stir together all the prepared ingredients except a little of the mashed chestnut. Add the yeast extract and a moderate seasoning of salt and pepper and mix to a rough paste. If very stiff, moisten with enough chestnut liquor to bring it to the consistency of dough (but do not add too much, as it is impossible to make tidy croquettes if the mixture is too runny. The idea of leaving a little mashed chestnut to be added at the end is a precaution against this). Stir in the rest of the chestnut.

**3** Set the oven to 200°C, 400°F, Gas Mark 6. Cut the crust from the bread and grate finely; remove any ragged scraps, which will cook unevenly. Put the crumbs on to one large plate; spread the flour, lightly seasoned with salt and pepper, on another; wash and break the egg on to a third; season very slightly with salt and pepper and beat smooth. Form the dough into flattened, thickish rounds the size of fish cakes and coat, first with flour, then egg, then crumbs. Shake off any surplus but ensure that each cake is completely covered.

**4** Line the baking tray with cooking foil and spread with the oil. Lay the croquettes a little apart and bake for 20 minutes, by which time the crumbs on the underside will have browned; turn and bake for a further 10-15 minutes, until brown and crisp on both sides. Serve with Cauliflower in Béchamel (see below).

# · CAULIFLOWER IN · BÉCHAMEL

Serve this with the Chestnut Croquettes on page 153. The sauce is flavoured with enough Gruyère cheese to give it zest but not to taste overwhelmingly cheesy; if necessary, substitute 1 oz/ 25 g Parmesan cheese.

If prepared directly the croquettes are in the oven, the cauliflower should be ready to bake when they are turned.

## · INGREDIENTS ·

| | |
|---|---|
| 1 *medium cauliflower* | *Scant ¼ teaspoon ground nutmeg* |
| *2 oz/50 g Gruyère cheese* | *Salt and pepper* |
| *½ pint/300 ml milk* | **Ovenware dish** |
| *½ oz/15 g butter or 1 tablespoon oil* | |
| *½ oz brown or white flour (brown makes a less smooth sauce)* | |

## · METHOD ·

**1** Remove leaves and cut any grey or brown patches from the cauliflower; divide into florets and wash. Put into a saucepan, half cover with water and add a pinch of salt. Bring to the boil and boil for 4-5 minutes, until just, but only just, tender. Drain immediately and arrange in the ovenware dish.

**2** Coarsely grate the cheese. Heat, but do not boil, the milk. Melt the butter or warm the oil in a saucepan over low heat, add the flour and stir until smooth. Immediately, but slowly, pour in the milk, stirring continuously. Continue stirring for 3-5 minutes until the sauce thickens. Remove from the heat. Season moderately with salt and pepper, stir in the cheese and sprinkle over the nutmeg.

**3** Pour over the cauliflower, making sure that all the florets are covered, and bake for 10-15 minutes, until beginning to brown.

# · CHICKEN WITH ORANGE ·
# AND BRANDY

Next to plain roast, this is the simplest way of cooking chicken I know – and, apart from the brandy (plus the fact that it needs accompaniments), it is also one of the cheapest.

The chicken can either be roasted whole or cut into portions; the first looks more impressive and saves the 5 or 10 minutes needed to divide it and set the stock to boil but the second is quicker to cook and, if an hour for simmering is allowed, can be accompanied by the pilaff on page 49.

With pilaff, serve a green salad to follow; otherwise serve this dish with plain rice (see page 46) and Watercress and Orange Salad (see page 158).

For 4 *or* 6, depending on the size of the chicken. With a 4½-5 lb/2.25-2.5 kg chicken, be sure to use the larger quantitites I have given.

## · INGREDIENTS ·

| | |
|---|---|
| *3½-5 lb/1.75-2.5 kg chicken* | **Salt and pepper** |
| *2 or 3 largish cloves garlic* | **Baking tray for a whole chicken or ovenware dish for portions** |
| *1 large or 2 small oranges* | |
| *1 tablespoon or 3 dessertspoons brandy* | **Sharp, smallish knife for cutting the portions** |
| *1 rounded tablespoon or 3 rounded dessertspoons thick honey* | |

## · METHOD ·

**1** Set the oven to 200°C, 400°F, Gas Mark 6. *If using a whole chicken*: remove the giblets (usually sold in a bag inside the bird) and keep the liver if the carcass is to be used for stock. Wipe the chicken inside and out with moistened kitchen roll, place breast upwards on the baking tray and season with salt and pepper. Put the chicken into the oven. Roasting times are 20 minutes per

1 lb/500 g plus 15 minutes for a 3½-4 lb/1.75-2 kg bird or 10 minutes for a 4½-5 lb/2.25-2.5 kg: thus 3½ lb/1.75 kg needs 1 hour 25 minutes, 4 lb/2 kg 1 hour 35 minutes, 4½ lb/2.25 kg 1 hour 40 minutes, 5 lb/2.5 kg 1 hour 50 minutes (these times are generous, but to avoid the risk of salmonella the chicken must be thoroughly cooked).

**2** Peel and chop the garlic; wash the orange(s); mix the brandy and honey to a thin paste. Roast the chicken until it has 45 minutes left to cook. Take it out of the oven, shutting the door so that heat does not escape, and finely grate the zest of the orange(s) over it; scatter with the garlic, spoon over the honey and brandy, and return to the oven. Baste after 10 minutes and subsequently every 10-15 minutes. When ready, the chicken will be coated with a dark, shiny glaze and the sauce will have turned a deep brown. Carve by cutting off the legs, twisting sharply (as when raw) to separate the joint at the bottom; halve the legs at the knee; slice the breast diagonally from the central breast-bone.

**3** *If using chicken portions, and to serve accompanied by pilaff*: divide the chicken at least 2¼ hours before serving: make the stock, prepare the pilaff ingredients, and fry the onion for the latter before putting the chicken into the oven. Use the meat from the carcass, not for the pilaff but Chicken in Béchamel (see page 86).

**4** To divide the chicken, remove the giblets from the chicken; reserve the liver. Wipe the bird inside and out with wet kitchen roll. Set it breast downwards and cut round the legs, keeping close to the ribs; separate the joint at the top (the thigh) with a twist. Turn the trunk over and slice off the breasts as near the breast-bone as possible. As in this instance crisp skin is desirable, try to cut the skin neatly without dislodging it (this is no problem with the legs but less easy over the breasts). Divide a larger bird into 6 by chopping the legs additionally at the knee joint.

**5** Set the oven to 200°C, 400°F, Gas Mark 6. Arrange the chicken pieces in the ovenware dish and season with salt and pepper. Wash and finely grate the orange(s) over them as above; peel, chop, and scatter garlic into the dish; mix and spoon the honey and brandy over each piece. Bake for 45 minutes, basting every 10-15 minutes as before.

# · WATERCRESS AND · ORANGE SALAD

The larger quantities are for 6, the smaller for 4.

## · INGREDIENTS ·

| | |
|---|---|
| 1 *bunch watercress* | 1 *large or 2 small oranges (the ones used for zest above)* |
| 2 *or 3 heads of chicory* | |
| 1-1 ½ *oz/25-40 g walnut pieces* | French Dressing (*see page 94*) |

## · METHOD ·

**1** Carefully pick over the watercress, throwing away discoloured leaves; trim the bottom of the stalks. Cut off the root end and remove the outer layer of leaves from the chicory; pull off the rest of the leaves, trimming off any withered tips or brown streaks, until near the heart; cut more from the bottom if necessary. Halve or quarter the heart. Wash and leave all leaves to drain.
**2** Roughly chop the walnuts and put to crisp in the oven (already hot because of the chicken) for 4-5 minutes.
**3** Set the chicory leaves, preferably unchopped, on individual plates; if there are enough, arrange in a star. Put the cress on top.
**4** Peel the orange(s), being careful to remove all pith; slice, cut the slices in half if desired, and place on the cress.
**5** Scatter the walnut over the orange. Make the dressing; spoon a little over each portion just before serving.

# · SPINACH AND PINE · NUT TART

Of all the possibilities with spinach, this is one of the most delicious; the combination of pine nuts and Parmesan cheese complement its bitterness and give it an intriguing smoky flavour, while the former also accentuate its nutty texture (which depends on cooking it for the minimum time necessary to soften it).

It is particularly suitable for parties because the filling is very compact, which means that there will probably be enough for 6; it will also slice tidily (8-12 slices) for a buffet meal.

Large-leaved, white-stemmed sea-kale beet can be used instead of spinach but has less flavour.

## ▪ INGREDIENTS ▪

| | |
|---|---|
| *1 lb/500 g spinach* | *1 egg, size 2* |
| *Salt and pepper* | *2 tablespoons milk* |
| *3 oz/90 g pine nuts* | *2 oz/50 g Parmesan cheese* |
| *1 small clove garlic* | **Largish saucepan with a lid** |
| *2 oz/50 g ricotta or similar medium-fat soft cheese* | **8½ inch/22 cm tart dish** |

## ▪ METHOD ▪

**1** Pick over the spinach, throwing away any very damaged leaves; cut out beet stalks. Wash, twice if necessary.

**2** Put the spinach in the saucepan with a little salt and 2 tablespoons water; with sea-kale beet, use 2 inches/5-6 cm. Cover and set over medium heat for 6-7 minutes or until submerged in liquid and tender; 10-12 minutes for beet. Turn into a colander and press out as much moisture as possible. Chop roughly.

**3** Set the oven to 180°C, 350°F, Gas Mark 4. Line the tart dish with the pastry.

**4** Roughly crush the nuts (this is easy, as they are quite soft); to add variation to the filling, leave a few whole, or almost whole.

**5** Crush the garlic in a pestle and mortar, then transfer to a bowl. Add the ricotta cheese, beat in the egg, and thin with the milk. Season very slightly with salt and a little more generously with pepper. Finely grate the Parmesan cheese, and stir in.

**6** Add the spinach and nuts and mix well. Spread in an even layer over the pastry, and bake for 25 minutes. Eat hot or cold.

# SAVOURY
## · PROFITEROLES ·

Like Gougère, these are made from choux pastry and are excellent as a main or first course at a sit-down meal. They also make a quicker, easier, and certainly equally popular alternative to vol-au-vents at parties. They can be served cold or hot (they take only 10 minutes to heat up) with a variety of fillings. Two alternatives, one cold (herb), one hot (leek), are given below; other possibilities are spinach, as for Gougère (see page 70) or mushroom (see page 66).

You will find the dough much easier to handle if it is chilled for a few hours beforehand or even overnight in the refrigerator. The recipe given here makes about 18 fair-sized buns (if this is too many, use two-thirds of the quantities, with pastry as for Chocolate Profiteroles, see page 138).

As precision matters, exact metric equivalents are given and should be adhered to.

### · INGREDIENTS ·

| | |
|---|---|
| 2½ oz/70 g white self-raising flour | ⅜ pint/220 ml water |
| 2 oz/60 g wholemeal flour | 3 eggs, size 2 or 3 |
| Salt and pepper | 2 oz/50 g strong Cheddar cheese |
| 3 oz/85 g butter | Extra white flour |

#### HERB FILLING

| | |
|---|---|
| Handful mixed fresh herbs, preferably including basil (a particularly good mixture is basil and marjoram with a little tarragon) or, if herbs are unobtainable, a bunch of watercress | 8 oz/250 g ricotta or other fresh-tasting medium-fat soft cheese |
| | Salt and pepper or, if using watercress, paprika |
| 2 oz/50 g strong Cheddar cheese | A little plain yoghurt if necessary to moisten the cheese |

## LEEK FILLING

| | |
|---|---|
| 1 lb/500 g leeks | ⅜ pint/220 ml milk |
| 1 tablespoon oil | 1 level teaspoon French mustard |
| ½ oz/15 g butter | 2 oz/50 g strong Cheddar cheese |
| ½ oz/15 g white flour | |
| **Baking sheet** | **Small saucepan** |

## ▪ METHOD ▪

**1** Mix the flours and season with a little salt and pepper. Put into a cup or mug. Chop up the butter and place in a small saucepan with the water. Heat gently until the butter has melted, bring to a vigorous boil, and tip in the flour. Turn off the heat and beat until the flour is incorporated into a smooth, stiff dough. Leave for a few minutes to cool.

**2** Break and beat in the eggs one at a time. Do not add the next until the first one is completely mixed in. After the addition of the first the dough will be almost as stiff as before, after the second softer, and after the third the consistency of thick cream. Chill if possible.

**3** Set the oven to 220°C, 425°F, Gas Mark 7. Grease the baking sheet. Finely grate the cheese. Put about a tablespoon of white flour on to a saucer for dusting the hands and mould the dough into balls about the size of walnuts; keep hands well floured. Place on the baking sheet far enough apart to allow for each to quadruple in size. Sprinkle with the cheese and bake for 20 minutes without opening the oven door. The profiteroles will have puffed up enormously and should be mid-brown; if still pale, bake for another 1-2 minutes.

**4** To *make the herb filling*: wash the herbs or watercress, pat dry on kitchen roll. Discard thick stems from the former (but not the cress), then chop as finely as possible. Finely grate the Cheddar, then mash it into the soft cheese with a fork; if the mixture is dry, add just enough yoghurt to moisten (pre-packed ricotta is sometimes quite crumbly rather than creamy). Season to taste. Make a slit in the side of each profiterole and spoon the filling into the cavity.

**5** To *make the leek filling*: cut the root and leaves from the leeks, slice very finely, wash, and rinse under the tap in a colander; shake to remove surplus liquid. Put into a frying pan or saucepan with the oil and butter, season lightly with salt and pepper, then fry very gently, stirring frequently, for 7-10 minutes or until soft but not brown. Stir in the flour, add the milk, and continue stirring until thick. Mix in the mustard and cheese. If the profiteroles are to be served immediately, set the oven to 190°C, 375°F, Gas Mark 5. Fill the profiteroles as above and reheat for 10 minutes.

# · CHEESE STRAWS ·

The quantities given make about 36 straws and you might as well make the full amount even for only a few people, since the straws are so light that it seems as if you are eating virtually nothing (in fact they are about 70 calories each).

Either the dough or the cut straws can be made a day in advance. Store unbaked in the refrigerator.

## · INGREDIENTS ·

| | |
|---|---|
| *6 oz/190 g strong Cheddar cheese* | *4 tablespoons cold water* |
| *8 oz/250 g white self-raising flour, or 4 oz/125 g wholemeal and 4 oz/125 g white* | *2 teaspoons French mustard* |
| | *2 oz/50 g butter straight out of the refrigerator* |
| *Salt and pepper* | *Extra flour* |
| *2 oz/50 g soft margarine* | |

## · METHOD ·

**1** Finely grate the cheese. Season the flour with a little salt and a generous sprinkling of pepper. Work with the margarine until the mixture is like fine breadcrumbs. Stir in the cheese. Mix the mustard and water, make a well and pour it in, and form into a dough. If it seems too dry, add a little more water.

**2** Cut the butter into 8 slices. Roll the dough into a thick oblong, dust with flour, place 2 slices of butter on one end, and fold over. Re-roll into another oblong and repeat 3 times. If possible, cool the dough in the refrigerator.

**3** Set the oven to 220°C, 425°F, Gas Mark 7. Roll out the dough about ¼ inch/0.5 cm thick into as neat and tidy an oblong as you can. Trim the edges straight and cut into strips about ½ inch/ 1.5 cm wide and 2-2¼ inch/5-6 cm long. Re-roll and cut the trimmings until all the dough is used.

**4** Line the baking sheet with cooking foil. Arrange the strips on it at least ⅓ inch/1 cm apart and bake for 12 minutes or until risen and golden brown.

# · FERNANDO'S PASSION · CAKE

In more prosaic terms, this is carrot cake — but it is not prosaic, since it is remarkably rich-tasting and, as it really should be made with olive oil as recommended by Fernando (a romantically handsome Brazilian), extremely expensive.

Similarly, Fernando used cream cheese for the icing and filling: curd could be substituted but does not suit the cake so well (skim-milk cheese should not be used unless the cake will be finished within 24 hours).

Lemon juice can replace brandy but the latter acts as a preservative (the cake will stay moist for at least a week).

## · INGREDIENTS ·

| | |
|---|---|
| 1 *lb*/500 *g carrots* | 4 *oz*/125 *g plain white flour* |
| 2 *oz*/50 *g walnuts or walnut pieces* | 2 *oz*/50 *g white self-raising flour* |
| ½ *pint*/300 *ml olive or sunflower oil* | 1½ *level teaspoons ground cinnamon* |
| 8 *oz*/250 *g dark brown sugar* | |
| 3 *eggs, size 3 or 4* | ½ *level teaspoon salt* |

| | |
|---|---|
| 1⅓ teaspoons baking powder | 4 oz/125 g sultanas |
| 1⅓ teaspoons bicarbonate of soda | 4 oz/125 g raisins |

**FILLING AND ICING**

| | |
|---|---|
| 1 lb/500 g cream cheese | 2 tablespoons brandy or the juice of 1 small lemon |
| 8 oz/250 g icing sugar | |

**8 inch/20 cm cake tin**

## ▪ METHOD ▪

**1** Set the oven to 150°C, 300°F, Gas Mark 2. Line the bottom of the cake tin with cooking foil and oil the tin, including the foil. Peel and coarsely grate the carrots; roughly chop or crush the walnuts or walnut pieces.

**2** Stir together the oil and sugar (they look horrible, but do not be put off). Add the eggs and beat until smooth.

**3** Blend the flours, cinnamon, salt, baking powder and bicarbonate of soda and add to the egg mixture.

**4** Stir in the walnuts, sultanas, and raisins, separating any lumps of fruit which have stuck together. Stir in the carrot. Transfer to the cake tin and bake for 1 hour 30 minutes or until a fine skewer inserted into the centre comes out clean. The cake should be dark brown: do not be misled by the colour into thinking that it is burnt. Leave on a wire rack until completely cold before adding the filling and icing.

**5** Using a sharp knife halve the cake horizontally; it is moist and crumbly so lift off the top half with a fish slice. With a fork, beat together the cream cheese, icing sugar and brandy or lemon juice. Use slightly less than half for the filling. The icing can either be spread thickly over the top or more thinly over both top and sides.

# Chocolate Sauce
## · for Ice Cream and ·
## Profiteroles

Chocolate Profiteroles can be turned into a suitably sticky pudding by replacing the icing with hot chocolate sauce — or the sauce can be served with Vanilla Ice Cream (see page 171), which in my view is much better than chocolate ice cream. Two versions are given: the first is richer and smoother and probably the more suitable with ice cream; the second, which is made with brown sugar, has a grittier texture and subtler flavour.

## · RICH CHOCOLATE SAUCE ·

### · INGREDIENTS ·

| | |
|---|---|
| 3½ oz/100 g cooking or plain chocolate | ¼ pint plus 2 tablespoons/ 200 ml water |
| 3 oz/90 g caster sugar | |

### · METHOD ·

1 Break up the chocolate and put in a saucepan with the sugar and water over low heat. Stir continuously until the chocolate has melted. Bring to the boil and simmer for 15 minutes or until thick. Serve hot or warm.

## · BITTER CHOCOLATE SAUCE ·

### · INGREDIENTS ·

| | |
|---|---|
| 3½ oz/100 g cooking or plain chocolate | 2 oz/50 g soft dark brown sugar |

| 1 *teaspoon instant coffee dissolved in* *2 tablespoons water* | *¼ pint/150 ml water* |
|---|---|

## • METHOD •

1 Melt the chocolate with the sugar and water as for Rich Chocolate Sauce. Bring to the boil, add the coffee and simmer for 25 minutes.

# • HAZELNUT MERINGUE • CAKE

As with chocolate profiteroles, cream makes the best filling. However, if you really must substitute a low-fat filling for cream, beat 4 oz/125 g Quark or other skim-milk cheese with the juice of half a lemon and sugar to taste.

The most popular fruit for the filling is raspberries; next in order of preference are pineapple, blackberries, and oranges. (Small pineapples are sometimes very cheap: if the leaves at the top can be pulled off fairly easily, they are ripe; if the fruit feels definitely soft, they are too ripe.)

Brandy, Cointreau or Kirsch add a touch of luxury to the cake, but are not essential.

## • INGREDIENTS •

| 4 oz/125 g ground hazelnuts | 8 oz/250 g caster sugar |
|---|---|
| 4 eggs, size 2 or 3 | Salt |
| **FILLING** | |
| ½ pint/300 ml double cream | 3 oz/90 g caster sugar |
| 8 oz/250 g raspberries, pineapple or blackberries, or 2 oranges | 2 tablespoons liqueur (very optional) |
| **Two 8 inch/20 cm cake tin bases and/or baking tray** | **Large bowl** |

## · METHOD ·

**1** Set the oven to 180°C, 350°F, Gas Mark 4 and line the baking tray with cooking foil; turn up the edges to make a rim if necessary. Toast the hazelnuts for 4-6 minutes or until pale brown, shaking at intervals. Leave to cool. Lower the oven to 110°C, 225°F, Gas Mark ¼. Line the cake tin bases with foil and grease thoroughly, or grease the foil used for the nuts on the baking tray.

**2** Separate the eggs. Wash (in case bits of shell fall into the whites) and break each one over an individual cup or bowl. Crack sharply in the middle and tilt the yolk from one half of the shell to the other until all the white has fallen out. (The yolks are not needed for the cake but can be used for ice cream: see page 171.) Transfer the whites to the large bowl.

**3** Add a pinch of salt and whisk until close-textured and stiff enough to hold their shape when twirled or dipped from the whisk. Whisk in half the sugar. Stir in the rest. Stir in the hazelnuts. Spoon half the mixture over each cake tin base, leaving a ½ inch/1.5 cm margin, or spoon in 2 circles on the baking tray. Bake for 1½ hours. Leave to cool.

**4** To make the filling, wash and leave raspberries or blackberries to drain while the meringue cooks; chop oranges or pineapple into small pieces. Add the sugar to the cream with the liqueur, if using, and whip until stiff. Chill in the refrigerator. Mix with the fruit and sandwich the meringue rounds just before serving. (The cream will make the meringue soggy if added too soon.)

# · MICHAEL'S FRUIT · SALAD

F‌ruit salad need not be as expensive as you might think — you can vary the ingredients according to price and season; as with stir-fries and other salads, however, a contrast of taste, colour and texture will give the best result.

You need at least two pieces of fruit, or 8 oz/250 g per person; for juice, use a 7 fl oz/200 ml carton fruit juice per 2 lb/1 kg (and add any juice which escapes from the fruit as it is cut up). Do not sweeten, but leave individuals who want sugar to add their own. In this recipe, the Conference pear adds crisp texture; the kiwi fruit may or not have much flavour, but looks beautiful, and the tropical fruit juice adds a hint of exotic flavour without costing more than most other juices. *For 4.*

## ▪ INGREDIENTS ▪

| | |
|---|---|
| ⅜ pint/200 ml tropical fruit juice | 1 Conference pear |
| 2 oranges | 2 Cox's apples |
| 4 oz/125 g black grapes | 1 banana |
| 1 kiwi fruit | |

## ▪ METHOD ▪

Pour the fruit juice into a bowl. Peel the oranges, using a sharp knife to remove all the pith, and cut across into slices. Wash, halve and pip the grapes. Peel and slice the kiwi fruit. Peel the pear and apples, if wished, otherwise wash, then slice. Add all the fruit to the juice in the bowl (the apples and pear must be added immediately or they will quickly discolour if left exposed for even only a short period). Peel and slice the banana and add to the bowl. Chill before serving.

# ▪ ICES ▪

Until very recently it was virtually impossible (in this country) to buy ices which tasted anything like the home-made version — and it is still safe to say that, if you can, they will be very expensive.

Without equipment, ices based on eggs, such as vanilla, are expensive anyway because they call for a high proportion of cream; fruit ices, however, need less or can be made with yoghurt, and are economical in that the fruit can be bought relatively cheaply in season: indeed, one of their recommendations is that they are perhaps the nicest way of preserving raspberries, strawberries, and other berry fruits.

Water- and low-fat ices with a professional texture can only be made with the aid of a machine to break up the ice crystals as they form (beating at intervals is a nuisance and will not achieve finer crystals than in *granita*, i.e. about the size of coffee sugar); with a moderate amount of cream or Greek yoghurt (rather than low-fat), however, one can produce perfectly smooth fruit ices with only one beating session or even none at all.

The ices should be frozen in plastic or similar containers with firmly-fitting lids: used ones from bought ices or other frozen foods are fine, or as a last resort freeze in a pudding-basin covered with food-wrap.

Storage time is 3 months; after this, flavour will deteriorate.

Allow 1-2 hours for deep-frozen ices to thaw; mix or beat with a fork before serving.

The quantities in the following recipes make about ¾ pint/450 ml, i.e. enough for 4-6.

# RASPBERRY AND
# · STRAWBERRY ICES ·

Raspberry is everyone's favourite (including mine) but ices are an advantageous way of using strawberries because, like tomatoes, they often have very little flavour and gain considerably from pulping with lemon and sugar.

## · INGREDIENTS ·

| | |
|---|---|
| 1 lb/500 g raspberries or strawberries | Squeeze of lemon juice |
| 4 oz/125 g caster sugar | ¼ pint/150 ml Greek or Greek-style yoghurt or double cream |

## · METHOD ·

1 Carefully pick over and wash the fruit; leave to drain.
2 Pulp with the sugar and lemon juice through a sieve. Add the pulp to the cream or yoghurt (rather than vice versa: with cream, unless very thick, it does not matter, but yoghurt will not mix in

at all well if it is added to the juice). Mix and for best results sieve again.

**3** Turn into a freezer container or pudding basin and freeze for 2-2½ hours or until the edges are frozen but the centre still soft (freezing times vary according not only to the temperature of the freezer but size and shape of the container). Whisk or beat with a fork until homogeneous and refreeze (this will give a slightly smoother result than without beating but is not essential). For immediate consumption, the ice will be ready after a further 1½-2 hours.

# · GOOSEBERRY, BILBERRY, · BLACKCURRANT AND DAMSON ICES

JUST as they make excellent jam, so damsons also make remarkably good ices: gooseberries are also especially recommended for their full flavour.

With damsons, 6 oz/190 g sugar is needed; for gooseberries, 5 oz/160 g; for bilberries and blackcurrants, 4 oz/125 g.

## · INGREDIENTS ·

| | |
|---|---|
| 1 lb/500 g fruit | ¼ pint/150 ml Greek or Greek-style yoghurt or double cream |
| 4-6 oz/125-190 g caster sugar | |

## · METHOD ·

**1** Pick over the fruit, removing any green bilberries or currants, and wash. Leave to drain.

**2** Put with the sugar (no water) over very low heat and sweat until the sugar has melted and the juice has started to run; turn up the heat slightly and stew for 5-6 minutes or until the fruit is soft and submerged in liquid (damsons will take 7-10 minutes). Allow to cool.

**3** Pulp through a sieve and proceed as in the previous recipe.

# · VANILLA ICE CREAM ·

Though the most basic, this remains one of the most delicious of all flavours of ice cream (provided a vanilla pod rather than essence is used); it is also a way of using up the egg yolks left over from meringues. Note, however, that because the eggs are not heated to a high enough temperature to kill bacteria, it is important to use a reliable source such as a large supermarket.

Vanilla pods can be bought at any good grocer or delicatessen: they are relatively expensive but can be used twice (as well as ice cream, they are excellent for yoghurt).

## · INGREDIENTS ·

| | |
|---|---|
| *1 vanilla pod* | *4 egg yolks, size 2 or 3 (for separating eggs, see page 142)* |
| *¼ pint/150 ml milk* | |
| *½ pint/300 ml double cream* | *4 oz/125 g caster sugar* |

## · METHOD ·

**1** Rinse the vanilla pod in cold water and score the surface lengthwise with a knife to release the seeds. Add to the milk and cream and heat, but do not allow to boil. Cover the pan (partly to keep the contents warm) and leave for 10-15 minutes to infuse. Remove the pod, rinse, and keep for future use.

**2** Beat the yolks and sugar until smooth and pour the milk and cream over them by degrees, stirring continuously. Set over very low heat and continue stirring for 3-5 minutes until the mixture starts to thicken; to begin with, it will be frothy or bubbly on top, but as it thickens the surface will become smooth. Immediately remove from the heat and stir a few more minutes. Pour through a sieve into a bowl, cover with a plate, and leave to cool.

**3** Transfer to a freezer container and freeze for 2-2½ hours, then beat and refreeze as before.

# WHEN YOU'RE
## ·REALLY BROKE·

WHEN I HEAR tales of people who by the end of term can afford only mashed potatoes and carrots for dinner, I feel that the whole of this book should have been on the financial level of this chapter — but in fact quite a lot of other recipes in the book might just as well have qualified for this chapter, including Kaity Karageorgis's Tsatziki and Hummus (see pages 11 and 13), Celeriac and French Onion Soup (see pages 19 and 21), Quick Chive Sauce (see page 31), Carrot and Walnut Tart (see page 42), Stir-fried Vegetables made with whatever vegetables are cheapest (see pages 50 to 57), Stuffed Marrow (see page 64), Cheese Soufflé (see page 68), Sydna's Bean and Spinach Salad (see page 96) and the Cheese and Walnut Breads (see pages 114 and 116), which, in nutritional terms at least, make the foundation of a meal: just add Green Salad of lettuce or runner beans.

The recipes given here are not only cheap but, with the exception of Gnocchi, quick (the end of term may mean not only shortage of money but exams). Several obvious possibilities have been excluded: macaroni cheese, for instance, is almost universally condemned as boring, and nobody needs a recipe for baked potatoes. An example of a cheap vegetable stir-fried dish is Polly's Carrot and Peanut Pasta; a general idea for saving is making your own yoghurt (as long as you resist the urge to add expensive flavourings) and muesli, and recipes for both of these are given in this chapter. Eat both together for a really economical and nutritious breakfast.

# · LENTIL AND CARROT · SOUP

This soup depends simply on the taste of the lentils, which is complemented and enhanced by the carrot. Serve with crusty bread. *For 3-4.*

## · INGREDIENTS ·

| | |
|---|---|
| *2 medium onions* | *1¾ pints/1 litre water* |
| *1 or 2 cloves garlic* | *6 oz/190 g split red lentils* |
| *8 oz/250 g carrots* | *Pinch of ground nutmeg* |
| *1 tablespoon oil* | *Salt and pepper* |

## · METHOD ·

**1** Peel and finely chop the onions and garlic; scrub or peel and coarsely grate the carrots.
**2** Fry the onions in the oil over gentle heat, turning often, for 10 minutes or until soft. Add the garlic and fry for 2-3 minutes. Stir in the carrot and continue frying for 5 minutes, turning the vegetables constantly.
**3** Add the water and lentils, bring to the boil, and skim. Boil for 10 minutes, then simmer for 25 minutes. Add the nutmeg, season to taste with salt and pepper, and serve.

# · POLLY'S CARROT AND · PEANUT PASTA

Although very economical, this is surprisingly rich-tasting (partly due to the yoghurt, which should be Greek or Greek-style). Its crunchy texture goes better with macaroni or largish pasta shapes than spaghetti-type pasta or rice.

Plain, roasted, or salted peanuts can be used according to preference (I favour roasted).

Use natural soy sauce, such as shoyu or tamari as it has a much better flavour. *For 2-3.*

## ▪ INGREDIENTS ▪

| | |
|---|---|
| ½ *small cabbage, weighing about 8 oz/250 g* | 1 *rounded teaspoon cornflour* |
| *Salt* | 5 *oz/150 g Greek or Greek-style yoghurt* |
| 8 *oz/250 g pasta quills, shells or macaroni* | 2 *tablespoons oil* |
| | 2 *oz/50 g peanuts* |
| 3 *carrots, weighing about 8 oz/250 g* | 1 *tablespoon soy sauce* |
| 1 *medium onion* | **2 large saucepans** |
| *Small sliver root ginger* | |

## ▪ METHOD ▪

**1** Halve the cabbage lengthwise and store the unwanted half in a food bag in the refrigerator. Discard the outermost leaves if damaged or flabby and the stalks. Chop the cabbage into ⅓ inch/1 cm squares and wash. Bring a saucepan of slightly salted water to the boil, add the cabbage, bring the water back to the boil, and boil for 2 minutes. Rinse under the cold tap and leave to drain.

**2** Cook the pasta in a saucepan of boiling salted water; time the pasta to be ready 5 minutes after starting to fry.

**3** Meanwhile, peel and slice the carrots into 1 inch/2.5 cm lengths; stand each length on end and cross-chop into matchsticks. Peel and finely chop the onion; peel the ginger and cut into 2 or 3 thin slices (only a little is needed). Blend the cornflour into the yoghurt.

**4** If the cabbage is still damp, blot dry with kitchen roll. Put all the prepared ingredients and the soy sauce within reach. Measure the oil into the second large saucepan and set over high heat until hot. Add the ginger and fry until slightly coloured. Put in the onion and stir for about 15 seconds; add the carrot and cabbage and stir for 2½ minutes. Stir in the nuts and soy sauce. Remove from the heat, wait a few seconds, then add the yoghurt. Drain the pasta and serve immediately with the vegetables.

# · GNOCCHI ·

I know that if I describe these as a kind of dumpling, nobody will want to try them. In fact, they are home-made potato pasta formed into tiny dumplings simply because this is the easiest way to shape them — shaping being the snag about them, since an amount sufficient for 4 will take one person nearly 30 minutes. I therefore suggest either making them for only 2-3 or (as with pounding peas for hummus) that the task of shaping is shared (forming the dough into sausages and cutting it across into discs is sometimes recommended, but I find the result so messy that the cakes have to be reformed into dumpling shapes, i.e. balls, anyway).

The recipe itself is very simple but, as in other similar cases, details matter — in this instance ensuring that the dough is sufficiently dry, that the gnocchi are simmered rather than boiled, and simmered for the right amount of time. Accompaniments can be any sort of sauce for pasta, but just Parmesan, plus a little butter, is surprisingly good (unfortunately for the cause of economy, Cheddar is less suitable, partly because it is not so strong but also because of the lack of textural interest which is given by the grittiness of Parmesan).

If possible, use floury potatoes, such as King Edward, Cara, Pentland Squire or Romano. The flour can be brown, white, or a mixture (the latter is recommended); as the larger amount is needed, an exact metric equivalent is given. *For 2-3.*

## · INGREDIENTS ·

| | |
|---|---|
| 1 lb/500 g floury potatoes | 1 egg, size 2 |
| Salt and pepper | 1 oz/30 g plain white flour |
| A large pinch, or ¼ teaspoon ground nutmeg | 1 oz/30 g wholemeal flour |

| | |
|---|---|
| About 1 oz/25 g (1 heaped tablespoon grated) Parmesan cheese plus a little more for serving if desired | A little extra flour (white) for shaping the gnocchi |
| | ½-1 oz/15-25 g butter |
| A few drops oil | **Shallow ovenware dish** |

## • METHOD •

**1** Peel, cut into equal-sized pieces, and boil the potatoes in slightly salted water for 20 minutes or until soft. Drain and mash with a fork over very low heat to dry them out; remove from the heat when the potato starts sticking to the edge of the pan but continue mashing until very smooth. Leave to cool.

**2** Season with the nutmeg, a very little salt, and rather more pepper. Break in the egg, mash smooth. Stir in the flour to make a stiffish dough.

**3** Set the oven to 200°C, 400°F, Gas Mark 6. Finely grate the cheese if necessary. Pour plenty of very slightly salted water into as large a saucepan as is available and add the oil (this helps to prevent sticking): put on to boil when about two-thirds of the dough is shaped. A large plate will be needed on which to put the gnocchi as they are formed — do not let them touch each other or they will stick together. Sprinkle a little white flour on to another plate for keeping the hands floured and shape the dough into marble-sized balls.

**4** Adjust the heat so that the water in the saucepan is just simmering. Use a fish slice to slide the marbles of dough into the water (with this number and a reasonably wide pan, they can all be cooked at once, but with quantities for 4 they should be simmered half at a time). The temperature of the water will drop when they are put in; cook for 4 minutes from when it returns to simmering (with gas, the flame can be raised for a moment or two). After 2 or 3 minutes, the gnocchi will rise to the surface, which theoretically means that they are cooked, but if removed at this stage they tend to taste of flour. Lift them out with the slice and pile into the ovenware dish (once cooked, they do not stick together). Dot with the butter, sprinkle with the Parmesan and put into the oven for 5 minutes, when the cheese will be melted, or 8-10 minutes when it will be slightly browned and crunchy. Eat with or without more cheese (personally, I do not think more is necessary).

# · TOAD-IN-THE-HOLE ·

This is much more attractive than anyone who has only tried the frozen version might imagine. Formerly, it was made either with steak or cold meat — with luck, enlivened by the addition of a few oysters; today, it can be given zest with interesting sausages.

The batter is similar to that for pancakes and, as with the latter, benefits enormously from being allowed to stand for an hour or so beforehand.

Do not use brown flour: with white, the pudding puffs up enormously like a soufflé and looks magnificent but with brown will remain flat and muddy-looking.

## · INGREDIENTS ·

| | |
|---|---|
| Salt | 8 oz/250 g (4 large or 8 small) sausages |
| 4 oz/125 g white self-raising flour | |
| 2 eggs, size 2 or 3 | Soufflé or pie dish |
| ⅜ pint/220 ml milk | |

## · METHOD ·

**1** Blend a generous pinch of salt into the flour, make a well in the centre and break in the eggs. Mix to a smooth, thick paste. Stir in the milk gradually, pressing out any lumps against the side of the bowl. Allow to stand.

**2** Set the oven to 220°C, 425°F, Gas Mark 7. Thoroughly grease the baking dish (this is in the interests of washing up, since lack of fat in the batter means that otherwise it will certainly stick). Prick the sausages, arrange in the dish and bake for 15-20 minutes or until beginning to brown; leave to cool for a few minutes.

**3** Stir and pour in the batter. Bake for 30 minutes; do not open the oven door during cooking. Serve immediately.

# · PEAS-IN-THE-POD ·

This is a vegetable version of Toad-in-the-Hole and was supposed to have been called Tadpoles-in-the-Hole: it was pointed out, however, that this was hardly a vegetarian name.

Although it rises less spectacularly than Toad-in-the-Hole, the taste of the vegetables permeates the whole pudding and makes it gastronomically far more interesting. *For 3-4.*

## · INGREDIENTS ·

| | |
|---|---|
| 4 oz/125 g white self-raising flour | 4 oz/125 g mushrooms |
| Salt and pepper | 8 oz/250 g fresh (unshelled) peas or 4 oz frozen |
| 2 eggs, size 2 | |
| ⅜ pint/220 ml milk | 1-1½ tablespoons oil |
| 1 large onion | ½ teaspoon mixed dried herbs |
| 2 cloves garlic | **Soufflé or pie dish** |
| 2 small courgettes | |

## · METHOD ·

**1** Season the flour moderately with salt and pepper, make a well in the centre and break in the eggs. Mix to a smooth, thick paste. Stir in the milk gradually, pressing out lumps of flour against the sides of the bowl. Leave to stand for at least 1 hour before continuing with the recipe.

**2** Set the oven to 220°C, 425°F, Gas Mark 7. Thoroughly grease the baking dish. Peel and finely chop the onion and garlic; wash and slice the courgettes about ⅓ inch/1 cm thick. Trim the stalks, then wash small or peel and wipe large mushrooms and slice finely. Shell the peas if necessary and boil for 5 minutes or until tender. Transfer to the dish.

**3.** Fry the onions in 1 tablespoon oil over gentle heat for 10 minutes. Add the garlic and mushrooms and fry for 5 minutes or until changing colour. Put into the dish with the peas. Add a little more oil to the pan, if necessary, and fry the slices of courgettes

with the herbs; turn the slices after 2-3 minutes or as soon as the first side browns. Add to the other vegetables in the dish.
**4.** Stir and pour in the batter. Bake for 35 minutes; do not open the oven door during cooking. Serve immediately.

# · BEANS GRATINÉ ·

This is cheap, filling, and fairly quick to make — but you have to remember to soak the beans in cold water overnight. It takes 1½ hours to cook. *Enough for at least* 4.

## · INGREDIENTS ·

| | |
|---|---|
| *6 oz/190 g each haricot and black-eyed beans, soaked in cold water overnight* | *4 oz/125 g Cheddar cheese* |
| *Salt and pepper* | *About ¾ oz/20 g or ½ a thick slice of stale brown bread for grating (fresh tends to form doughy lumps)* |
| *1 lb/500 g ripe tomatoes* | **Largish ovenware dish 3-4 inches/7.5-10 cm deep** |
| *1 large onion* | |
| *1 tablespoon oil* | |
| *1½ level tablespoons tomato paste plus 1 tablespoon water* | |

## · METHOD ·

**1** Drain and rinse the beans, put them into a saucepan with enough water to cover, boil briskly for 10 minutes, then simmer for a further 30 minutes. Add ½ teaspoon salt and continue simmering for 10-20 minutes or until the haricot beans are soft.
**2** Meanwhile, skin and chop the tomatoes, discarding the cores; peel and finely chop the onion. Fry the onion gently in the oil for 7-10 minutes or until soft. Add the tomato and simmer for a further 10 minutes, pressing out lumps of flesh against the bottom of the pan. Mix the tomato paste with the water, add to the pan and continue simmering for a further 5 minutes or until the sauce is thick. Set the oven to 200°C, 400°F, Gas Mark 6.

**3** Coarsely grate the cheese and finely grate the bread, keeping them separate.

**4** Drain the cooked beans and transfer to the ovenproof dish. Cover with the tomato, add an even layer of cheese, and sprinkle with the breadcrumbs. Bake for 25 minutes or until the breadcrumbs are crisp and the cheese melted.

# · POTATO SOUFFLÉ ·

This is a much more filling soufflé than Cheese Soufflé (see page 68). Use floury potatoes, such as King Edward, Cara or Pentland Squire. Serve with watercress, if possible. *For 3-4.*

## ▪ INGREDIENTS ▪

| | |
|---|---|
| *1 lb/500 g potatoes* | *Salt and pepper* |
| *6 oz/190 g strong Cheddar cheese* | **Egg whisk** |
| *4 large eggs* | **8½ inch/21 cm soufflé dish or other ovenware dish of similar diameter and at least 4½ inches/11 cm deep** |
| *3 teaspoons French mustard (e.g. Grey Poupon)* | |
| *3 tablespoons milk* | |

## ▪ METHOD ▪

**1** Peel the potatoes, put into a large saucepan, and boil in slightly salted water for 20 minutes or until soft. Drain and mash with the mustard, milk, a light seasoning of salt, and plenty of pepper. Leave to cool a little. Coarsely grate the cheese and stir it in.

**2** Set the oven to 200°C, 400°F, Gas Mark 6. Grease the soufflé or other dish. Separate the eggs. Wash (in case pieces of shell fall into the whites) and break each one over a separate cup or bowl. Crack briskly in the middle and tip the yolk from one half of the shell to the other until all the white has fallen into the cup. Drop the yolks into the saucepan of potato; transfer the whites to the large bowl.

**3** Add a pinch of salt to the whites and whip until stiff enough to hold their shape when twirled or dropped from the whisk.
**4** Fold (very gently stir) the whites into the potato mixture. Spoon carefully into the dish and immediately put into the oven. Bake for 40 minutes without once opening the oven door. Serve immediately.

# · CHICK PEA AND TUNA · SALAD

Not many recipes have every virtue, but this is one — it is cheap, remarkably nutritious, and, apart from soaking and cooking the peas, very quick. *For 3-4.*

## ▪ INGREDIENTS ▪

| | |
|---|---|
| *12 oz/375 g chick peas, soaked in cold water overnight* | *1 bunch spring onions* |
| *Small bunch parsley (enough for 2 tablespoons when chopped)* | *7 oz/200 g can tuna fish in brine* |
| *French or Lemon and Tomato Dressing (see pages 94 and 95)* | |

## ▪ METHOD ▪

**1** Rinse the chick peas in cold water and pick out any discoloured ones. Cover with unsalted water, bring to the boil, skim, and simmer for 1 hour; top up the water if necessary. Add a little salt and continue simmering until the chick peas break easily with a fork. Meanwhile, wash the parsley and leave to drain.
**2** Drain the chick peas. Make the dressing and pour it over them while they are still warm.
**3** Cut off the root end and green leaves from the spring onions; peel off the outer layer and slice. Drain the tuna; finely chop the parsley. Mix the tuna with the peas and scatter the parsley and onions over the top.

# · POTATO AND EGG ·
# SALAD

This salad is quick to make but needs to be left for a few minutes to allow the eggs and potatoes to cool and steep in the dressing before serving.

For the potatoes, choose Maris Bard, Piper, Ulster Sceptre, Desirée or Pentland Crown rather than the flourier King Edward, Cara or Pentland Squire. *For 4.*

## · INGREDIENTS ·

| | |
|---|---|
| 1 lb/500 g new potatoes | 4 oz/125 g hard cheese |
| Salt | Small handful basil |
| 4 eggs | 2 or 3 parsley sprigs |
| Garlic Dressing (see page 95) | |

## · METHOD ·

**1** Scrub the potatoes, removing any patches of green, and cook in boiling salted water for 15-20 minutes until just soft. In a separate saucepan, boil the eggs for 12 minutes. Make the dressing.

**2** Slice the eggs and potatoes as soon as they are cool enough to handle, put into the salad bowl, and cover with the dressing.

**3** Dice the cheese and add to the bowl. Wash the basil and parsley and leave to drain.

**4** Just before serving, finely chop the herbs and toss into the salad gently (vigorous tossing may break the pieces of potato).

# · YOGHURT ·

Since the ingredients for a pint of yoghurt (without flavourings) are a pint of milk and a tablespoon of yoghurt, you can make your own for hardly more than the cost of the milk — which means a saving of over 100%. Not much work is involved — but, as with bread, and for the same reason (to allow living organisms to reproduce), warmth and time are needed (in this case 6-8 hours). Unlike ices, plain yoghurt will not differ markedly from the commercial product since its quality depends largely on that of the yoghurt used as a starter. However, an enormous difference can be made by adding your own flavourings.

The only equipment you need is a saucepan, spoon and heatproof bowl such as a pudding basin, plus a larger bowl and towel for insulation. As not only the yoghurt but other bacteria flourish in warm milk, you need to sterilize the equipment by rinsing with boiling water. This recipe uses U.H.T. (long-life) milk, which is already sterilized. If you want to use ordinary milk, you will need to sterilize it by simmering it for 10 minutes (by which time it will taste the same as U.H.T. milk).

The only requirements for the yoghurt used as a starter are that it should be natural, fresh (i.e. not near the end of its sell-by date) and unpasteurized — which, far from applying only to yoghurts specifically described as 'live', in fact includes nearly all the brands on sale: any which are pasteurized will be labelled so.

Use low- or full-fat milk according to which kind of yoghurt you want (the starter yoghurt can also be either). *For just over* 1 *lb*/500 *g* (4 *servings*).

## ▪ INGREDIENTS ▪

| | |
|---|---|
| 1 *pint*/600 *ml* U.H.T. *milk* | **Large bowl** |
| 1 *tablespoon natural yoghurt* | **Towel** |
| **Pudding basin or similar bowl** | |

## ▪ METHOD ▪

**1** To sterilize the equipment, fill a saucepan with water (it should hold enough to fill the basin in turn). Put in a tablespoon. Bring to the boil, boil for about 1 minute, then quickly pour the water into the basin; also transfer the spoon (use a cloth, as the handle may be hot). Let the water stand in the basin for a few minutes. Empty, leaving the spoon, and allow the basin to cool, preferably until it is still lukewarm to the touch rather than completely cold.

**2** Put the yoghurt into the basin and stir until smooth with the sterilized spoon. Pour the milk into the saucepan, wash your hands (because of the need to test its temperature) and heat the milk until it feels positively warm but not hot (ideally, it should be 42°C/106°F: a little deviation on either side does not matter, but if it is much hotter, the yoghurt may curdle, and if much cooler, little will happen and the yoghurt will be unsatisfactorily thin). Mix 1 tablespoon of the milk with the yoghurt, then pour in the rest slowly, stirring continuously. Continue stirring for a moment or two, then cover with a plate. Set the basin in the bowl. Using a teapot, pour into the side of the bowl enough water of about the same temperature as the mik to come three-quarters of the way up the basin; take care not to add too much or it will overflow into the yoghurt. Wrap in a towel and leave in a warm place for 6-8 hours, until the yoghurt is set. Do not leave to stand any longer, or the yoghurt may be very sharp to the taste or (as when the milk is too hot) even curdle. If the basin is still warm, let it cool by standing it in cold water for a while. Cover and store in the refrigerator.

**3** The yoghurt will keep for up to 4 days and can be used as a starter for a new batch during the first 2 days (if it is older, contamination by foreign bacteria is more likely). It should be replaced as a starter by commercially made yoghurt after 3 batches.

**Variations** To make flavoured yoghurt, use any of the flavourings given below. All the flavourings except rhubarb and vanilla, which have to be left to infuse, can be prepared in a matter of minutes; they taste better, however, if left for 30 minutes or so for the flavour to develop. The vanilla flavouring needs to be added before the yoghurt is made, all the rest are added afterwards.

The quickest — honey — needs no comment except to say that, although more difficult to mix, you should opt for thick honey over the runny sort because the latter will make the yoghurt altogether runnier in consistency; the quantity needed is about 3 tablespoons.

# · RASPBERRY AND STRAWBERRY ·

## · INGREDIENTS ·

| | |
|---|---|
| 8 oz/250 g strawberries or 6 oz/ 190 g raspberries | Squeeze of lemon juice with strawberries |
| 3 oz/90 g caster sugar or to taste | |

## · METHOD ·

Pick over and wash the fruit, then leave to drain. Chop the strawberries, if using, mix with the sugar, then leave for 2 or 3 minutes for the juice to run; add with the lemon juice to the yoghurt. If using raspberies, sprinkle with the sugar and leave for a few minutes to become soft and juicy; lightly crush with a fork and mix with the yoghurt.

# · BANANA ·

## · INGREDIENTS ·

| | |
|---|---|
| 2 bananas | 3 oz/90 g soft brown sugar |

## · METHOD ·

Mash the bananas with the sugar, then mix with the yoghurt.

# · BANANA AND MUESLI ·

## · INGREDIENTS ·

| | |
|---|---|
| 1 banana | 3 oz/90 g demerara sugar |
| 6 oz/190 g muesli | |

## · METHOD ·

Mash the banana with a fork and add to the yoghurt with the muesli and sugar.

# · Vanilla ·

Use a fresh vanilla pod (available from grocers' and delicatessens) rather than essence. The pod must be heated with the milk before the yoghurt is made. It can be used twice.

## · INGREDIENTS ·

| | |
|---|---|
| 1 *vanilla pod* | 1½-2 oz/35-50 g *white sugar* |

## · METHOD ·

Rinse the pod in cold water and score the surface lengthwise with a knife. Add to the milk, bring to the boil, and leave to cool for 15-20 minutes or until just warm. Remove the pod and (unless it has been used before) wash and keep for future use. Proceed with the yoghurt. Add sugar to taste after it is made.

# · Lemon ·

## · INGREDIENTS ·

| | |
|---|---|
| 3 oz/90 g *white sugar or to taste* | *Juice of* ½ *large or* 1 *small lemon* |

## · METHOD ·

Mix the sugar with the yoghurt, then add the lemon juice. Add more sugar, if needed.

# · Rhubarb ·

To my taste this is even better than raspberry.

## · INGREDIENTS ·

| | |
|---|---|
| 1 *lb*/500 g *rhubarb* | 1 *tablespoon water* |
| 6 oz/190 g *soft brown sugar* | |

## • METHOD •

Trim the root ends and cut off the leaves, and peel or scrape any brown streaks from the surface of the rhubarb stalks. Wash and chop into ⅓ inch/1 cm lengths. Put in a saucepan with the sugar and water over very low heat until the sugar has melted and the juice has started to run. Raise the heat slightly and stew for 20-25 minutes to a thick purée (if not cooked until thick, the yoghurt will be too runny). Leave until cold and mix with the yoghurt.

# • MUESLI •

Since manufacturers can buy wholesale and muesli is a relatively low-priced product, the saving on making your own is not going to be great — and, as with yoghurt, can easily be cancelled out by additions. The following, however, is about 15% cheaper than an average commercial basic mixture — which if one or several people eat it every day is enough to be well worth making the effort.

The malted wheat is crunchy and adds a hint of sweetness.

As the peanuts (which should be plain) do not need chopping, making it hardly takes 5 minutes.

## • INGREDIENTS •

| | |
|---|---|
| 2 oz/50 g sunflower seeds | 4 oz/125 g crushed wheat grains |
| 12 oz/375 g rolled oats | 4 oz/125 g raisins |
| 6 oz/190 g malted wheat flakes | 4 oz/125 g plain peanuts |

## • METHOD •

Toast the sunflower seeds in a frying pan over highish heat, shaking frequently so that they heat evenly, for 2-3 minutes or until they start to change colour. Continue to toast, shaking constantly until they are an even golden brown. Mix with all the other ingredients and store in an airtight jar.

# NUTRITION

As given in the *Manual of Nutrition*, Ministry of Agriculture, Fisheries and Food, Her Majesty's Stationery Office, 9th ed., recommended daily requirements for men and women aged 18-34 are:

**Men:** moderately active:

Energy 2,900 kcal; protein 72 g; calcium 500 mg; iron 10 mg; vitamin A 750 $\mu$g; thiamin 1.2 mg; riboflavin 1.6 mg; niacin equivalent 18 mg; vitamin C 30 mg.

Very active:

Energy 3,350 kcal; protein 84 g; minerals and vitamins as above.

**Women**: moderately active:

Energy: 2,150 kcal; protein 54 g; calcium 500 mg; iron 12 mg (on average); vitamin A 750 $\mu$g; thiamin 0.9 mg; riboflavin 1.3 mg; niacin equivalent 15 mg; vitamin C 30 mg.

Very active:

Energy: 2,500 kcal; protein 62 g; thiamin 1.0 mg; minerals and other vitamins as above.

Anyone eating a normally mixed diet with plenty of fresh foods probably receives more than enough of everything, but, as meat and fish are major sources of protein, vegetarians need to consider this aspect of their intake especially.

Proteins are made up of amino acids in different proportions and arrangements. Animal proteins are more similar to man's than vegetable and therefore, taken singly, more useful; the utility of plant proteins, however, can be increased by eating several sorts more or less at the same time. A proportion of dairy products (animal) is obviously helpful.

Quantitatively, a day's requirements can be met by (for instance): ½ pint/300 ml milk; a generous bowl of muesli; 2-4 oz/50-125 g cheese; a pot of yoghurt; an egg; 2 oz/50 g of either red kidney beans or peanuts or a serving of spinach plus 4 oz/125 g lentils; 4-6 thick slices of wholemeal bread.

As packaged foods are labelled with their nutritive value, the following table consists chiefly of items likely to be bought loose; mineral and vitamin content are excluded, but dairy produce, soya and kidney beans, and rhubarb are particularly rich in calcium; butter, margarine, carrots, and lettuce in vitamin A; green peppers, Brussels sprouts, blackcurrants, oranges, lemons, and strawberries in vitamin C; watercress in calcium and vitamins A and C; spinach in calcium, iron, and vitamins A and C (and also protein).

## FOOD VALUES

Figures from the *Manual of Nutrition* except where marked *

| Per 100 g: | Energy kcal | Protein g | Fat g | Carbo g |
|---|---|---|---|---|
| **MEAT** | | | | |
| Beef (minced, stewed) | 229 | 23.1 | 15.2 | 0 |
| Chicken (roast, with skin) | 213 | 24.4 | 12.8 | 0 |
| Chicken (roast, without skin) | 148 | 24.8 | 5.4 | 0 |
| Pork chop (cooked, with fat) | 332 | 28.5 | 24.2 | 0 |
| Pork sausage (cooked) | 317 | 13.6 | 24.5 | 11.2 |
| **FISH** | | | | |
| Cod, haddock, plaice | 77 | 17.1 | 0.9 | 0 |
| Herring (whole) | 251 | 16.8 | 20.4 | 0 |
| Mackerel | 282 | 19.0 | 22.9 | 0 |
| **DAIRY PRODUCE** | | | | |
| Eggs | 147 | 12.3 | 10.9 | 0 |
| Milk (whole) | 65 | 3.2 | 3.9 | 4.6 |
| Milk (skimmed) | 32 | 3.4 | 0.1 | 4.7 |
| Cheddar cheese | 406 | 26.0 | 33.5 | 0 |
| Butter | 740 | 0.4 | 82.0 | 0 |
| **GROCERIES** | | | | |
| Sugar (white) | 394 | 0 | 0 | 105.3 |
| Flour (wholemeal) | 306 | 12.7 | 2.2 | 62.8 |
| Bread (wholemeal) | 215 | 9.0 | 2.5 | 41.6 |
| Rice (brown, boiled)* | 160 | 3.5 | 1.5 | 36.0 |
| Spaghetti (raw) | 342 | 12.0 | 1.8 | 74.1 |

## NUTS (SHELLED), SEEDS, AND PULSES

| | | | | |
|---|---|---|---|---|
| Almonds | 565 | 16.9 | 53.5 | 4.3 |
| Hazelnuts* | 665 | 16.1 | 65.1 | 7.2 |
| Peanuts | 570 | 24.3 | 49.0 | 8.6 |
| Walnuts* | 630 | 16.0 | 56.6 | 15.0 |
| Sunflower seeds* | 582 | 24.0 | 47.3 | 16.0 |
| Sesame seeds* | 582 | 18.6 | 49.1 | 17.5 |
| Lentils (cooked) | 99 | 7.6 | 0.5 | 17.0 |
| Kidney beans | 272 | 22.1 | 1.7 | 45.0 |

## VEGETABLES

| | | | | |
|---|---|---|---|---|
| Aubergine | 14 | 0.7 | 0 | 3.1 |
| Beans (runner, boiled) | 19 | 1.9 | 0.2 | 2.7 |
| Cabbage (raw) | 22 | 2.8 | 0 | 2.8 |
| Cabbage (boiled) | 15 | 1.7 | 0 | 2.3 |
| Carrots | 23 | 0.7 | 0 | 5.4 |
| Cauliflower (cooked) | 9 | 1.6 | 0 | 0.8 |
| Celery | 8 | 0.9 | 0 | 1.3 |
| Courgettes (raw) | 29 | 1.6 | 0.4 | 5.0 |
| Cucumber | 10 | 0.6 | 0.1 | 1.8 |
| Lettuce | 12 | 1.0 | 0.4 | 1.2 |
| Mushrooms | 13 | 1.8 | 0.6 | 0 |
| Onion | 23 | 0.9 | 0 | 5.2 |
| Parsnips (cooked) | 56 | 1.3 | 0 | 13.5 |
| Peas (boiled, frozen) | 72 | 6.0 | 0.9 | 10.7 |
| Peppers (green) | 12 | 0.9 | 0 | 2.2 |
| Potatoes | 74 | 2.0 | 0.2 | 17.1 |
| Spinach | 30 | 5.1 | 0.5 | 1.4 |
| Tomatoes | 14 | 0.9 | 0 | 2.8 |
| Turnips (cooked) | 14 | 0.7 | 0.3 | 2.3 |
| Watercress | 14 | 2.9 | 0 | 0.7 |

## FRUIT

| | | | | |
|---|---|---|---|---|
| Apples | 46 | 0.3 | 0 | 11.9 |
| Avocado pear | 223 | 4.2 | 22.2 | 1.8 |
| Bananas | 76 | 1.1 | 0 | 19.2 |
| Blackcurrants | 28 | 0.9 | 0 | 6.6 |
| Lemon juice | 7 | 0.3 | 0 | 1.6 |
| Oranges | 35 | 0.8 | 0 | 8.5 |
| Rhubarb (cooked, with sugar) | 45 | 0.5 | 0 | 11.4 |

# INDEX